thegoodwebguide

holiday travel online

GW00716702

www.thegoodwebguide.co.uk

thegoodwebguide

holiday travel online

Arabella Dymoke

The Good Web Guide Limited • London

First Published in Great Britain in 2002 by The Good Web Guide Limited
Broadwall House, 21 Broadwall, London, SE1 9PL

www.thegoodwebguide.co.uk

Email:feedback@thegoodwebguide.co.uk

10 9 8 7 6 5 4 3 2 1

A catalogue record for this book is available from the British Library.

ISBN 1-903282-322

Project Editor Michelle Clare

Design by Myriad Creative Ltd

Printed in Italy at LEGO S.p.A.

contents

the good web guides

The World Wide Web is a vast resource, with millions of sites on every conceivable subject. There are people who have made it their mission to surf the net: cyber-communities have grown, and people have formed relationships and even married on the net.

However, the reality for most people is that they don't have the time or inclination to surf the net for hours on end. Busy people want to use the internet for quick access to information. You don't have to spend hours on the internet looking for answers to your questions and you don't have to be an accomplished net surfer or cyber wizard to get the most out of the web. It can be a quick and useful resource if you are looking for specific information.

The Good Web Guides have been published with this in mind. To give you a head start in your search, our researchers have looked at hundreds of sites and what you will find in the Good Web Guides is a collection of reviews of the best we've found.

The Good Web Guide recommendation is impartial and all the sites have been visited several times. Reviews are focused on the website and what it sets out to do, rather than an endorsement of a company, or their product. A small but beautiful site run by a one-man band may be rated higher than an ambitious but flawed site run by a mighty organisation.

Relevance to the UK-based visitor is also given a high premium: tantalising as it is to read about purchases you can make in California, because of delivery charges, import duties and controls it may not be as useful as a local site.

Our reviewers considered a number of questions when reviewing the sites, such as: How quickly do the sites and individual pages download? Can you move around the site easily and get back to where you started, and do the links work? Is the information up to date and accurate? And is the site pleasing to the eye and easy to read? More importantly, we also asked whether the site has something distinctive to offer, whether it be entertainment, inspiration or pure information. On the basis of the answers to these questions sites are given ratings out of five. As we aim only to include sites that we feel are of serious interest, there are very few low-rated sites.

Bear in mind that the collection of reviews you see here are just a snapshot of the sites at a particular time. The process of choosing and writing about sites is rather like painting the Forth Bridge: as each section appears complete, new sites are launched and others are modified. If you register at the Good Web Guide site you can check out the reviews of new sites and updates of existing ones, or even have them emailed to you.

By registering at our site, you'll find hot links to all the sites listed, so you can just click and go without needing to type the addresses accurately into your browser.

All our sites have been reviewed by the author and research team, but we'd like to know what you think. Contact us via the website or email feedback@thegoodwebguide.co.uk. You are welcome to recommend sites, quibble about the ratings, point out changes and inaccuracies or suggest new features to assess.

You can find us at
www.thegoodwebguide.co.uk

user key

£	Subscription
R	Registration Required
🔒	Secure Online Ordering
UK	Country of Origin
ab	ABTA Member
at	ATOL Member
ia	IATA Member

introduction

As Britons, we spend more on holidays and travel than anything else you can buy on the web. So it is little surprise that travel is the largest and fastest growing ecommerce category bringing the entire industry into your home or office. The internet has become the key channel for consumers and the new technologies have dramatically changed the whole experience.

The choice today is unparalleled, with access to a far greater inventory than anything the old economy could offer, with the added incentive of better prices. Consumers have the ability to purchase tickets and holidays when and where it suits them. The travel industry has always been information heavy, relying on brochures but the internet has removed the need for such publications. Consumers can now search the web and compile their own brochures on screen and even print a hard copy.

This is a constant changing industry with exciting new developments, yet to be fully exploited. Versions of web technology can be delivered via digital TV and WAP mobile phone. Some airlines allow their customers to check in from their office or via mobile phone. Others operate ticketless flights where a credit card number has sufficient information to let you board. It will not be long before everybody adopts this method.

Brand loyalty in online travel is notoriously low and so as consumers, we are ideally placed to benefit from the swashbuckling that the travel operators are going to have to engage in in order to become leaders in the field. Ten per cent of online air travel shoppers buy after visiting one site while 60 per cent visit two or three before committing themselves.

But why is travel such a huge growth area in the internet world? Travel arrangements have been a difficult thing to orchestrate at the best of times, pulling all the strings together from train and flight timetables to hotel reservations and foreign currency. The internet enables you to do this literally at the click of a button. You can be sure that information is up to date and you are able to compare what's on offer from accessing one page alone. The travel portals are literally the gateway to the world.

What about using your credit card online? It is, in fact, the safest method of payment as your credit card number is encrypted and is virtually impossible for anyone to intercept and decipher. But if you follow these ground rules, you should not go to far wrong. Firstly, ensure that the site is secure. Look for a locked padlock symbol, which you will find at the bottom of your web browser, usually in the right-hand corner. If you are concerned, ring the company. Every site should at least have a terrestrial address, telephone and fax number. Check to see if the company is ABTA protected. As a consumer you will get your money back if the company goes bust. If a company sells air tickets, it must hold an Air Travel Organisers' Licence. This protects you from losing money but also prevents you from being stranded abroad.

Keep hard copies of all your electronic correspondence. Print out the booking confirmation and any emails. Make a note of your booking reference number. But most of all, follow your instinct.

The internet does not always offer the cheapest alternative but without doubt costs are being reduced as booking procedures are improved. Also we still like to talk and to be at the receiving end of the personal touch. The internet allows you to explore all the possibilities that travel can offer before streamlining your choices. Before you switch your computer on, it does help to know what sort of holiday or flight you are after. However good a travel portal portends to be, it is only as good as the person operating it.

A word of warning: most of the sites listed in this book are key players in the travel industry but change is inevitable. Some will expand, others will merge or fall by the way side. You will have access though to the latest news and reviews by registering at www.thegoodwebguide.co.uk to receive your free online updates. The world is literally at your feet and you are but a click away from the excitement that travel can bring.

Arabella Dymoke,
March 2002

Travel Portals

Think of the word portal and Dr. Who and his tardis immediately come to mind. The tardis, small on the outside and vast on the inside, was capable of whisking Dr. Who forwards and backwards in time and to wherever he pleased at the click of a button. Travel portals have almost the same capabilities, offering a gateway to the rest of the web, and providing a window on the world and the travel opportunities on offer. A travel portal is a directory of links to other sites, offering many services, such as search engines online booking facilities, email links and chat rooms where travellers can exchange stories.

We have included several portals all doing the same thing but in a variety of styles and ways. Our advice is to have a look at them all and then choose just one that you like. Expedia is one of the most popular but you may prefer something a little more streamlined, such as eDreams.

overall rating:	★ ★ ★ ★ ★
classification:	e-agent
updated:	realtime
navigation:	★ ★ ★ ★ ★
content:	★ ★ ★ ★
readability:	★ ★ ★ ★ ★
speed:	★ ★ ★ ★ ★

UK   at   ab   ia

www.a2btravel.com
a2btravel.com

One of the biggest online travel agencies in the UK, this comprehensive site is now owned by the Online Travel Organisation. Offering all the services of a full-blown online agent, such as transportation, accommodation and information through links to other well-known sites, it has a pleasant European bias. The world's airlines appear in A-Z format with links to each. The site now has a more sophisticated image.

Eurotunnel, Eurostar and ferries timetables are large features of the homepage. Whilst the site offers worldwide possibilities, it is best-suited for travellers with varying pocket depths to, from and around the Continent. Skiing and snowboarding holidays to Europe and North America are also covered.

SPECIAL FEATURES

UK Mapping gives detailed maps for anywhere in the UK.

Brochures allows you to order from the UK's top holiday companies, free and online.

UK Airports tells you how to get to the airport by car, bus or rail and it is possible to book parking.

Overall a very strong site for those interested in travelling around Europe. Good for bargain hunting.

http://travel.americanexpress.com
American Express Travel

This established site is very slick. Its usefulness to UK users is questionable since holiday packages are sourced from the US. The flight search is fast. Details of the aeroplane (such as capacity and engine) is a rather neat feature within this facility.

SPECIAL FEATURES

Destination At A Glance pulls together city highlights from the ten most popular cities (courtesy of Fodor and 360 Virtual Tours), together with offers and savings.

Travel Tools provides Flight Tracker and Currency Converter.

Much to look at.

overall rating:	★ ★ ★ ★ ★
classification:	e-agent
updated:	realtime
navigation:	★ ★ ★ ★ ★
content:	★ ★ ★ ★
readability:	★ ★ ★ ★
speed:	★ ★ ★ ★ ★

US   at   ab

overall rating: ★ ★ ★ ★ ★	

overall rating:
★ ★ ★ ★ ★

classification:
e-agent

updated:
realtime

navigation:
★ ★ ★ ★ ★

content:
★ ★ ★ ★

readability:
★ ★ ★ ★ ★

speed:
★ ★ ★ ★ ★

UK   at   ab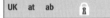

www.ebookers.com
Ebookers

Ebookers recently usurped both Expedia and Travelocity to become Europe's most popular European online agent. It offers the same package of all travel-related services and booking capabilities. Again, this site is large but after a little while, one easily gets the hang of it and it downloads information quickly. Discount fares and holidays are a strong feature. Travel Bazaar helps the traveller find all the necessary kit without hitting the High Street.

SPECIAL FEATURES

Multichannel is an innovative service getting flight information to your mobile or personal computer.

Fare alert lets you know if the price of a particular journey falls below your preferred level.

This seems to be an advanced online system. Users will be very happy with the slick service provided.

www.edreams.com
eDreams

eDreams is a site that aims to provide a broad range of holidays suited to all tastes, as well as information and advice to help you plan your perfect holiday. It offers a selection of 'hand-picked' holidays that can be browsed by selecting Activity (such as honeymoons or active journeys) or Destination (clicking on a region). Although the head office is in Barcelona, eDreams does have an office in London and is ABTA and IATA registered. Slow download times continue to dog this site, but the content is worth waiting for.

SPECIAL FEATURES

Tour Offers will find you a picnic in the desert on a four wheel drive safari in Dubai, or a night cruise in Hong Kong harbour on a traditional Chinese junk. If you prefer something a little tamer with a touch of culture, plump for their tours of Barcelona, or the volcanic island of Santorini.

Guides sets this site apart from other travel sites. It provides travel guides (called DreamGuides) who can answer questions and provide local information on a destination, from finding you accommodation or restaurants to providing suggestions on what to see and whether it is safe to travel to that place. Each guide also provides a list of links to websites that cover their area of expertise.

overall rating:
★ ★ ★ ★ ★

classification:
e-agent

updated:
realtime

navigation:
★ ★ ★ ★

content:
★ ★ ★ ★ ★

readability:
★ ★ ★ ★ ★

speed:
★ ★ ★

UK   ab   ia

Dream maps will advise you on where you can go in the world on your budget. With £200 to spend on a flight and the United States on your wishlist, Dream maps will come up with several suggestions.

A great first stop, particularly if you want a holiday with a difference. This is a classy site with information to match.

www.expedia.co.uk
Expedia

Owned by Microsoft, Expedia is one of the UK's oldest and largest travel-related sites, and is constantly updated and modified. It aims to give visitors the ability to find and book the right trip (including tickets, hotel rooms, car rentals, or full vacations) at the crucially important best price. The problem is definitely not the content but the size of the site, which can seem overwhelming.

Expedia is a capable and reliable agent directed at the mainstream traveller looking for straightforward arrangements at competitive prices. It generally favours efficiency at the cost of imagery but in this case, that's a good thing.

The homepage is so full of titles, links and symbols that it can be difficult to navigate. Use the Site Map for the simplest way to find your way around.

SPECIAL FEATURES

Expedia To Go downloads flight information to your mobile or pocket PC.

My Itineraries gives travellers the opportunity to register for personalised travel services, which can store travel itineraries or track low fares to three frequently used destinations. It remembers personal details such as home airport and has a

overall rating:
★ ★ ★ ★ ★

classification:
e-agent

updated:
realtime

navigation:
★ ★ ★ ★

content:
★ ★ ★ ★

readability:
★ ★ ★ ★

speed:
★ ★ ★ ★

US   at   ab   ia

mileage minder, which keeps frequent travel information in one place. If you're going to use the site often, persevering with the one-off membership sign-in is definitely worth it.

Fare Tracker lets you choose three favourite destinations and Expedia will find the best deals, emailing you the results.

Fare Compare shows fares other customers have found on a particular route.

Arrivals and Departures is an easy-to-use service, giving access to up-to-the-minute information.

360 Tours (under Destinations) allows you to tour the Serengeti Plain or the Taj Mahal to name but two.

Expedia is one of the most popular online agents and rightly so.

www.lastminute.com
Lastminute

Lastminute certainly showed the way in spontaneous travel and entertainment and their rivals duly followed suit. However, their aim is to encourage their customers to live out their dreams at unbeatable prices. Lastminute has managed to negotiate some favourable rates with hotels and airlines but the site's competitors now offer the same value-for-money trips. The site design lacks sophistication and has the looks of a teenage magazine but the information is all there. The quickest way to get to grips with what this site has to offer is to use the scroll-down site index on the left. The search facilities are excellent, with a running commentary on how your search is proceeding.

SPECIAL FEATURES

Auctions where you can bid for holidays or even DVD players and scooters, but you must register first.

Experiences suggests a myriad of activities to keep the adrenaline pumping or others for just chilling out. Check out Boys Toys and drive a Ferrari at Silverstone.

More can book taxis, find bargain weekends, and can help broke students find fares that even they can afford.

A quirky site for young and flamboyant eccentrics with a flexible schedule.

overall rating:
★ ★ ★ ★ ★

classification:
e-agent

updated:
realtime

navigation:
★ ★ ★ ★ ★

content:
★ ★ ★ ★ ★

readability:
★ ★ ★ ★

speed:
★ ★ ★ ★ ★

UK R at ab ia

overall rating:

classification:
e-agent

updated:
realtime

navigation:

content:

readability:

speed:

US   R   at   ab

www.mytravelguide.com
MyGuide Network

This American site sees itself as an active thriving travel community where members and guides share their travel experiences. It is currently under reconstruction and it appears that flight and accommodation booking have taken second place to the guides.

SPECIAL FEATURES

Ask a Question allows you to send emails to virtual guides on a number of subjects.

World Almanac provides information on countries with maps, geography, local economy, and people, with links through to related sites.

World Clock (under Tools) allows you to check on the time, by clicking on a time zone, on a map of the world. The clock, however, did not register British Summer Time.

Travel Videos requires membership, which is free.

A useful site for researching destinations.

www.otc-uk.com
Online Travel Company

Founded in 1998, Online Travel Company provides all travel and travel-related services for the leisure and corporate traveller. OTC can come up with the answers to your travel queries. The holidays they offer cover all price ranges.

Enjoy the videos of some of their chosen destinations.

SPECIAL FEATURES

iPoints is a rewards system, whereby valued customers receive ten iPoints for every £100 they spend. These can then be redeemed for a vast range of goods, which includes flights, holidays and shopping vouchers. Registration is necessary for this scheme.

Travel Extras is a series of links covering Insurance, Foreign Currency, Holiday Reading and Travel Guides (courtesy of Amazon).

An excellent site and if in doubt you can always call on the 150-strong customer support team.

overall rating:
★ ★ ★ ★ ★

classification:
e-agent

updated:
frequently

navigation:
★ ★ ★ ★ ★

content:
★ ★ ★ ★ ★

readability:
★ ★ ★ ★ ★

speed:
★ ★ ★ ★ ★

| UK | R | at | ab | ia | |

overall rating:
★ ★ ★ ★ ★

classification:
e-agent

updated:
regularly

navigation:
★ ★ ★ ★ ★

content:
★ ★ ★ ★

readability:
★ ★ ★ ★ ★

speed:
★ ★ ★ ★ ★

UK R at ab 🔒

www.opodo.co.uk
Opodo

Opodo has been created by nine of Europe's leading airlines and aims to become the leader of online booking in Europe by 2004. There is little to doubt that they will indeed achieve this target, and at the same time force prices down yet further, creating the most competitive market that there has ever been in the travel industry.

With access to flights from 480 airlines, 54,500 hotels and car rental from more than 23,500 locations worldwide, they have much to offer. Launched in January 2002, first impressions are good, although it looks unlikely that they will be able to match the knock down fares that the budget airlines are offering.

SPECIAL FEATURES

Travel Guides provides all the information on your chosen destination, from what to see and where to eat.

Travel Manager organises your travel arrangements, saves planned itineraries, and past bookings.

Opodo is a site to watch.

www.teletextholidays.co.uk
Teletext Holidays

How things have changed since Teletext on television was considered to be the height of cool. The service offered on its website is still the same but with all the trimmings that the 21st Century can bring. The holidays offered are in the lower budget bracket.

Look at the Site Map first to see all that is on offer and you will get a feel for the scale of this site. Once you've got to grips with it all, use the Shortcuts button, in the top right-hand corner, to move around the site. However, that done it is then difficult to return to the homepage.

SPECIAL FEATURES

Flight Directory is a basic service that does turn up some good deals. Dialaflight.com features strongly here (see p.68 of the air travel section).

Foreign Office Travel Alerts is found within the advice section, and is an abridged version of the alerts that they issue.

Set up Alerts will text message your mobile phone (for Vodafone users only) with information on holidays that meet your requirements.

Easy to use and for those who have moved from Teletext to the internet, this site will be the natural progression.

overall rating:	★ ★ ★ ★ ★
classification:	e-agent
updated:	daily
navigation:	★ ★ ★ ★
content:	★ ★ ★ ★
readability:	★ ★ ★ ★ ★
speed:	★ ★ ★ ★ ★

UK   at   ab

overall rating: ★ ★ ★ ★
classification: e-agent
updated: daily
navigation: ★ ★ ★ ★
content: ★ ★ ★ ★
readability: ★ ★ ★ ★
speed: ★ ★ ★
UK   at   ab 🔒

www.thomascook.co.uk
Thomas Cook

This newly re-launched site has all the marks of the Thomas Cook image, meeting all your travel requirements. The homepage is ordered and easy to follow, with three main features: Flights, Late Deals and Sun Holidays. The site highlights Thomas Cook TV, their new travel shopping channel broadcast on Sky. The Flight search turned up some interesting possibilities, with a very expensive flight from Stansted to Nîmes via Amsterdam. Have they not heard of Ryanair?

SPECIAL FEATURES

Foreign Exchange gives access to the virtual bureau, allowing you to order currency between the value of £200 and £2,000, which can be delivered to your door.

Destination Info is a comprehensive searchable travel guide with sensible information and recommendations.

The service offered by Thomas Cook is akin to talking to an aged relation: you will get reliable advice.

www.travelocity.co.uk
Travelocity

Owned by travel database group SABRE, this site offers a full online agency capable of booking transportation and accommodation for UK customers. It also offers access to a vast database of destination and other travel-related information. Download time has been improved and a graphics-free option is available if you want more speed.

To book, online registration (a 30-second deal) is required. But for those visiting the site in the name of research, entering as a visitor is a twice-available option.

Remember that dot-com and dot-co.uk access two different sites. Be wary of returning to the dot-com site, after accessing some of the pages, especially after using the Guide section, as you can easily lose your way.

SPECIAL FEATURES

Fare Watcher will track the lowest price on your chosen destination and will email you with updates. Registration is necessary for this service.

Next Weekend presents the weary and overworked with some good ideas for getting away. Especially suitable for those who aren't used to splashing out.

overall rating:
★★★★

classification:
e-agent

updated:
daily

navigation:
★★★

content:
★★★★

readability:
★★★★

speed:
★★★

US R at ab ia

Bed and Breakfast Directory (under Tools on the DreamPlanGo page) will help you find a place to stay in friendly surroundings in the US and Canada.

Traveller Advice gives reviews from some of Travelocity's happy customers, good if you are looking for that personal touch.

Dream Plan Go helps you plan your holiday. Choose a destination and information from some of the world's best travel guides will appear, along with holiday suggestions.

Site Tools, found in the upper right-hand corner of the homepage, allows visitors to register and access their personalised file.

Custom Miniguides (under Tools on the DreamPlanGo page) builds a personalised travel guide to featured destinations, to print and take with you.

Not much difference between this and Expedia. Go with one and stick with it. Jumping ship will prove a waste of time.

www.travelselect.com
Travel Select

Based in London, Travelselect was developed by Globepost Limited who, for years, have specialised in providing travel services to agents. Now they have expanded to include this online retail business.

In general, it offers flights, hotel accommodation and car rental worldwide, travel insurance and currency. It also offers a direct link to Eurostar's site for reservations and booking, but for other train journey information, visits to another site are necessary.

SPECIAL FEATURES

Fare Seeker is a new information service, which allows you to name your price for a flight and then fare seeker will notify you when they have found a flight that matches your requirement.

Multi-City Journey is directed at those with other than standard-return journeys to help them research and book tickets for the journey.

This site is not overwhelming and looks very user-friendly, although it may lack the weight in content of some of its rivals. If simplicity is what you are after, here's your site.

| overall rating: |
| ★ ★ ★ ★ ★ |

| classification: |
| e-agent |

| updated: |
| realtime |

| navigation: |
| ★ ★ ★ ★ ★ |

| content: |
| ★ ★ ★ ★ ★ |

| readability: |
| ★ ★ ★ ★ ★ |

| speed: |
| ★ ★ ★ ★ |

| UK   R   at   ab   🔒 |

overall rating: ★ ★ ★ ★ ★	
classification: e-agent	
updated: regularly	
navigation: ★ ★ ★ ★ ★	
content: ★ ★ ★ ★ ★	
readability: ★ ★ ★ ★ ★	
speed: ★ ★ ★ ★	

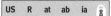
US   R   at   ab   ia

www.travelstore.com
travelstore.com

This relaunched site is a new slimline and fitter version of the old one, with emphasis on the business travel sector. In haste, at home or the office, you can buy air tickets, book hotels, hire a car, buy insurance, read the latest travel news, buy a travel guide, calculate currency changes, get travel points, print out itineraries and purchase records. The homepage is top-tabbed with every service category. These are quickly reached and very simple to use. When looking for savings, make sure to choose 'bargain hunter' as your search by option. Registration is required only when you make a booking.

SPECIAL FEATURES

Travel Guides links you to short guides that are jam-packed with activities and sightseeing opportunities as well as information for business-trippers. They even include the radio frequencies for the BBC and the VOA.

Corporate Accounts allows for expenses and itinerary tracking for a number of travelling employees.

Travel Links offers choices for train services, ferry services, visa information, time zone checks, airport guides, travel health and advice, as well as weather and currency information.

A quality, no-frills site that is simple to use.

www.travelweb.com
Travelweb

For an online agent, TravelWeb has the hippest and most dotcom-style homepage to date. The graphics, which consist of childlike drawings and writing in chalk colours on a black background, don't exactly shout 'Take us seriously, we are grown up and established', but navigating the site is child's play. This won't appeal to the silver surfers.

The site offers two services: a link to Expedia (see p.21) for flight reservations and a link to Hoteldiscounts for hotel reservations.

SPECIAL FEATURES

Click-it! Weekends offers deals from participating hotel chains from around the world. Prices are published every Monday, and they promise to be the lowest of the low but you do have to scroll down the list, which is arranged alphabetically by country.

TravelWeb's strength is Click-it! Weekends; why bother with the rest?

overall rating:
★ ★ ★ ★

classification:
e-agent

updated:
realtime

navigation:
★ ★ ★ ★

content:
★ ★ ★ ★

readability:
★ ★ ★

speed:
★ ★ ★ ★ ★

US

overall rating: ★ ★ ★ ★ ★	

classification:
e-agent

updated:
daily

navigation:
★ ★ ★ ★ ★

content:
★ ★ ★ ★

readability:
★ ★ ★ ★ ★

speed:
★ ★ ★ ★ ★

UK R   at   ab 🔒

www.worldof.net/travel
WorldOf.net

This busy site features a startling one million last-minute holidays and flights, and claims to be one of the largest collections of online travel information for the UK traveller. Content is growing rapidly and has just about every possible type of travel under its belt, from low-budget travel to a tailor-made option. The homepage, despite all the information listed, is manageable and easily navigable. Register for newsletters and special offers. All pages have a printer-friendly version.

SPECIAL FEATURES

Cheap Flights did have some difficulty finding suitable flights. Whilst searching, a small window with flashing adverts appears – irritating yes, but at least you know the engine is doing its bit.

City Breaks will find you a well-earned rest and with the Resort Guides, you can depart with some local knowledge already in your pocket. Ordering brochures is just a click away.

My Brochure creates a personal brochure, allowing you to compare prices. Registration is necessary for this facility.

Wedded Bliss suggests various locations for that special day, with comprehensive information on the resorts offered.

A user-friendly site for holiday searches and bookings but perhaps not so user-friendly for flights.

www.worldtraveldirect.com
WorldTravelDirect

All www.utravel.co.uk traffic is now directed to www.worldtraveldirect.com or www.wtd.com. This travel agent is geared towards the bargain end of the market, providing all the usual services of an e-agent. Registration is necessary immediately. The homepage is simple and uncluttered, just click on a symbol and off you go.

SPECIAL FEATURES

Red Light Flights is a great feature. When the symbol is flashing, you can get two air tickets for the price of one. How often this actually happens is not clear but it is something to keep a lookout for.

E-witness allows you into the world of the acclaimed travel writer, Marion Fox, and her knowledge of travel. There are some interesting articles here on new hotels, events and destination reports.

Activity Holidays has some good suggestions. Fancy a Harley Davidson tour in the United States? Or how about going whale watching? Take a look here.

A good-looking site which has quite a bit to offer. However, it lacks the busy-ness that its competitors have and leaves you feeling, what am I missing out on here?

overall rating:
★ ★ ★ ★ ★

classification:
e-agent

updated:
realtime

navigation:
★ ★ ★ ★ ★

content:
★ ★ ★ ★

readability:
★ ★ ★ ★ ★

speed:
★ ★ ★ ★

UK   R   at   ab   ia

OTHER SITES OF INTEREST

Holiday Choice
www.holidaychoice.co.uk

This site lists the principle tour operators that fly each leisure route. Type in a resort name and then you will be presented with a list of companies that operate in that area, with links through to their sites. Along with Flight Search, Hotel Deals and Late Availability, Holiday Choice offers much the same as its competitors. The service is swift and the site user-friendly.

Internet Travel Service
www.its.net

ITS is one of the leading travel website designers and their site is part advertisement to attract new customers and part travel portal. The site covers a broad range of travel categories, providing links to specialist companies.

Orbitz
www.orbitz.com

This site is very big in America and has received much press since its launch in June, 2001. Backed by the top five US airlines, Orbitz promises cost-cutting airfares that Expedia and Travelocity just won't be able to match. The site is easily navigable and searching for flights and holidays is fast and efficient. Keep an eye out for this one.

Travelgate
www.travelgate.co.uk

This directory has more than 2,000 links, which includes major tour companies and some less well-known ones. It covers cookery holidays to opera, canal holidays to villas in the sun. The homepage is crammed with links but is easy to use. The search facility is efficient.

TravelWorld
www.travel.world.co.uk
The largest index of European travel agents and tour operators on the internet. Having no American operators, it is mostly relevant for those in Europe or with an interest in Europe. The homepage is very plain, with nothing to jazz it up, just good plain information. Very easy to navigate.

World of Travel
www.worldoftravel.co.uk
An E-agent offering the same services as its competitors but lacking in style. The Late Availability feature presented very little information on a last-minute week's holiday in Tunisia, expecting you to book there and then. The site has been refined in that advertising has been all but removed. Maybe it will improve with time.

TRAVEL FOR THE DISABLED

All Go Here
www.allgohere.com
This site incorporates Everybody.co.uk. It gives a comprehensive listing of all disabled friendly airlines, UK hotels and services. The site is old-fashioned but the information is spot on.

Can Be Done
www.canbedone.co.uk
Can be done caters in holidays for the independent-minded traveller, in Europe, Scandinavia and North America, focusing on tours for those who prefer to plan their own itineraries. They have personal experience of the difficulties that travelling can present to people with disabilities, and make every effort to provide the same facilities for everyone, wherever feasible.

Tour Operators

These sites enable you to research your holiday and find the tour operator who can match your requirements. Using the internet also means that you can do away with wading through tons of brochures. Most sites, however, do allow you to order brochures online, if you are feeling old-fashioned.

overall rating:
★ ★ ★ ★ ★

classification:
tour operator

updated:
seasonal

navigation:
★ ★ ★ ★ ★

content:
★ ★ ★ ★

readability:
★ ★ ★ ★

speed:
★ ★ ★ ★ ★

FR	R	at	ab	

www.clubmed.com
Club Med

An easy-to-use site with a fun style, in keeping with the Club Med village atmosphere. Browse the site by using the search button, choosing a village by region, interest or ideal getaway. Or select a resort by sports & activity interests. The site map is a little more sedentary and you may get a feel for the content much faster by clicking straight onto this. Online booking is now possible, but you can always resort to the telephone if you need more information.

SPECIAL FEATURES

Village Life features animated sequences of all that Club Med offers, from its Dream Locations to Kids Kids Kids, complete with music.

Renovation gives news of the 73 villages that have been overhauled in the past few years, and of the current work in progress.

Great Deals is a quick way to find out what's on offer.

Take a Tour gives you a virtual tour of their village in Morocco, which is useful if you want to check out all the facilities.

A fun site encompassing the Club Med image.

www.elysianholidays.co.uk
Elysian Holidays

There are two approaches to this site. Either specify a holiday property preference: categories include Properties with Pools, Romantic/Honeymoon Hideaways, and Beach Houses. Alternatively, choose a holiday destination from a choice of Greece, Spain and Portugal, the Caribbean, or Cyprus. The site design could do with a makeover but the information is all for the taking. Booking is by email only.

SPECIAL FEATURES

Visitor Comments gives you a feel of the villas and services that Elysian Holidays offer.

Landscape & People gives information on some of the activities you can enjoy, such as riding, joining in with the locals at harvest-time, and walking. If you really want to get a feel for the place, local people welcome guests into their homes.

A personal site pioneered by Maxine Harrison, the founder of Elysian Holidays. It is a must for those with an interest in the Mediterranean or Caribbean.

overall rating:
★ ★ ★ ★

classification:
tour operator

updated:
seasonal

navigation:
★ ★ ★ ★ ★

content:
★ ★ ★ ★

readability:
★ ★ ★ ★

speed:
★ ★ ★ ★

UK at

overall rating:	
★ ★ ★ ★ ★	

classification:
tour operator

updated:
regularly

navigation:
★ ★ ★ ★ ★

content:
★ ★ ★ ★ ★

readability:
★ ★ ★ ★ ★

speed:
★ ★ ★ ★ ★

UK   at   ia

www.exodus.co.uk
Exodus

Exodus is one of the UK's leading gold medal winning adventure tour operators, with more than 25 years of experience. The site offers adventure holidays in more than 80 countries across Asia, Africa, the Americas, Antarctica and Europe.

The pages give concise and enticing summaries of their holidays, which are clearly organised on the homepage by type of adventure. Almost everything interlinks with everything else, so the lack of a site map is not a problem. Online booking is not available, though it's simple enough to book by phone.

SPECIAL FEATURES

Late Getaways lists holidays that usually depart within a week to a month and are very reasonably priced. The site links to full details of each trip and to similar trips that can be booked further in advance.

Holiday Finder is useful to sort holiday options by date, region, type of activity, and price.

Online Slide Shows is a selection of the company's favourite images. Flash software is required before the show can be downloaded.

A world-class, adventurous site.

www.just.co.uk
Just

Just is part of the Thomson Travel Group, and therefore has years of holiday experience under its belt. Choose your holiday destination by clicking on Hotel Info or Destination Info and Just will do the searching. Suggested holidays are all in the lower price range (starting from £140), and all can be booked online. If you have a fixed budget you can use the tabs running down the right-hand side of the page to choose a holiday by price.

Destinations tend to be those staples of the British package holiday, concentrating on the Canary Islands, the Costa Del Sol and Greece.

Information on resorts and maps are also given.

SPECIAL FEATURES

How to Use this Website tells you how to search for a holiday in four easy steps.

Budget holidays on an efficient site.

overall rating:

classification:
tour operator

updated:
daily

navigation:

content:

readability:

speed:

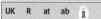

www.kuoni.co.uk
Kuoni

This household-name site gives information on the thousands of holidays they offer in 55 exotic countries. Online booking is possible for some but not all of the destinations offered. For the other non-online booking locations, a telephone number is given. The site is well-designed, making it easy for visitors to locate their subject of choice.

Registration offers any UK resident priority notification of special offers as soon as they become available. Complete a questionnaire and they will send only information that applies to you.

SPECIAL FEATURES

Create and Book Your Dream Holiday allows you to search for that perfect destination, by clicking on a world map.

Latest News has news of special offers.

Travel Extras links up with Kuoni's key travel partners in providing airport parking, online currency, and car hire.

Weddings & Honeymoons gives information on the 23 countries where Kuoni can arrange your wedding. Unfortunately, booking isn't possible online, but you can register for the weddings brochure or email for a personalised response.

This site exudes all the confidence that Kuoni offers.

www.thomson.co.uk
Thomson Holidays

overall rating:	★ ★ ★ ★ ★
classification:	tour operator
updated:	regularly
navigation:	★ ★ ★ ★
content:	★ ★ ★ ★
readability:	★ ★ ★ ★ ★
speed:	★ ★ ★ ★ ★

UK   at   ab   ia   🔒

This site is slick and easy to use. After all, Thomson Holidays have been responsible for sending millions of Britons abroad every year. They offer a wide range of holidays, run the most punctual charter airline, and there is a rep in each resort that they operate in.

Online booking is available, with a 24-hour telephone backup.

SPECIAL FEATURES

Our Holidays offers the full range from Platinum – a Deluxe holiday, to Superfamily – focusing on families with children up to the age of 12. At the bargain end, you can specify the destination, and Thomson chooses the accommodation.

Our Best Deals list discounted holidays and Cruises.

You know what you are getting with Thomson, and their site offers the same high standard.

overall rating: ★ ★ ★ ★	

classification:
tour operator

updated:
daily

navigation:
★ ★ ★ ★

content:
★ ★ ★ ★

readability:
★ ★ ★ ★

speed:
★ ★ ★

UK at 🔒

www.lunnpoly.com
Lunn Poly

The busy homepage will have you reaching for your sunglasses even before you have decided where to go. All the colours of the rainbow appear on the homepage. You can hitch a ride on the rotating last-minute deals or seek Agent Lisa's help to choose a holiday. Despite the garish colours, the site is entertaining.

SPECIAL FEATURES

The site is divided into several different sections that allow you to choose your holiday by type, and include: Sun Holidays, Villas, UK Holidays, Ski and Cruises.

Foreign Exchange is a virtual Bureau de Change that enables you to order between £50 and £2000 in foreign currency, with the money (either banknotes or traveller's cheques) delivered straight to your door. The sterling amount is adjusted to the nearest foreign banknote denomination, and charged to your credit/debit card.

There is not much here that sets this site apart but Lunn Poly are a long-established company, providing a reliable service. What's wrong with that?

www.markwarner.co.uk
Mark Warner

A very user-friendly site. The Mark Warner Club holidays are broken down into catalogue divisions such as summer, ski, singles and couples, and late offers. Family holidays are a speciality, and the company takes pride in the high quality childcare that they offer. Use the simple menu bar at the top of the homepage to reach them.

The site is attractive, but is perhaps best-used as an information source. Email your requirements and the company aim to contact the customer within two working days to discuss booking requests (others promise 24 hours). It is probably easier to phone at your own convenience.

SPECIAL FEATURES

Summer offers beach holidays, with plenty of watersports options, in ten Mediterranean locations.

Special Offers has information on last-minute deals for both families and individuals. The discounts offered are not jaw-dropping in their generosity. Look elsewhere for bargains.

An attractive online brochure with vacations for the young professional and for families.

overall rating:	★ ★ ★ ★ ★
classification:	tour operator
updated:	regularly
navigation:	★ ★ ★ ★ ★
content:	★ ★ ★ ★ ★
readability:	★ ★ ★ ★ ★
speed:	★ ★ ★ ★ ★

UK   at   ab

overall rating: ★ ★ ★ ★	

overall rating:
★ ★ ★ ★

classification:
tour operator

updated:
daily

navigation:
★ ★ ★ ★ ★

content:
★ ★ ★ ★

readability:
★ ★ ★

speed:
★ ★ ★ ★

UK   at   ab   ia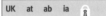

www.packyourbags.com
Pack Your Bags

Part of the well-established Country Trails Travel, this company specialises in holidays in areas that you might not even have thought of visiting. Want to hunt down Dracula or get off the beaten track in Eastern Europe? Packyourbags.com will come up with the goods.

The unsophisticated homepage belies the content of this site.

SPECIAL FEATURES

Design your own (under Holidays) lets you be the master of your own destiny. Fill in the form with your requirements and details, and Packyourbags.com will give you some suggestions.

Accommodation allows you to search for the perfect holiday home. The choice is extensive as you can choose from 20,000 properties on offer.

Round the World Offers can design a tailor-made itinerary for you at competitive prices.

Worth a detour.

www.seasonsinstyle.com
Seasons in Style

This smart, easy-to-navigate site offers luxury, tailor-made holidays to a collection of the finest hotels in the world. These include the tried and tested international chains such as the Hyatt and Four Seasons, but also extend to local independent establishments. They try and emphasise when to go, as well as where to go, believing the former to be an intrinsic part of your holiday's potential enjoyment value. The side bar on the homepage is rather small but despite that, navigation around the site is easy. It's definitely not for those with shallow pockets.

Email your booking requirements.

SPECIAL FEATURES

Luxury Plus invites visitors to book a special offer holiday, which doesn't mean a discounted week, just a great hotel and location.

Ideal Good Caution is a colour-coded grid which appears on each resort page and refers to the best times, weather-wise, to visit the country. However, the caution rating is somewhat underused, and for example, ignores the Monsoon season in the Far East.

If you like to travel in style and are prepared to pay the price, then this site is a must-see.

overall rating:
★ ★ ★ ★ ★

classification:
tour operator

updated:
occasionally

navigation:
★ ★ ★ ★ ★

content:
★ ★ ★ ★ ★

readability:
★ ★ ★ ★

speed:
★ ★ ★ ★

| UK | at | ab | ia |

overall rating:
★ ★ ★ ★ ★

classification:
tour operator

updated:
daily

navigation:
★ ★ ★ ★

content:
★ ★ ★ ★

readability:
★ ★ ★ ★

speed:
★ ★ ★ ★ ★

UK at ab

www.virginholidays.co.uk
Virgin Holidays

The design of this site feels so dated: the drab corporate colours of grey and red are akin to the uniforms of a cheap supermarket chain. The site certainly doesn't lift the spirit and there is no 'Oh yes' factor. But don't despair, you can expect to find lots of information, delivered speedily, and up-to-the-mark online booking facilities that you might expect in a Richard Branson venture.

The site is easy to use but you may have some trouble in returning to the homepage once you have chosen a destination. Click on the yellow Virgin Holidays' luggage label and you will return to the homepage immediately. The site is light on cultural information but then you have the specialist sites for those.

SPECIAL FEATURES

Get in the Mood is to be found under the Caribbean section, and lets you tune into Calypso music.

There are lots of savings to be made, so click away.

OTHER SITES OF INTEREST

Abercrombie and Kent
www.abercrombiekent.co.uk
A great site from the pioneers of luxury holidays to exotic and inaccessible places. Safaris are a speciality (see also pp.136, 139).

Airtours
www.airtours.com
This site is a gateway to the many companies that Airtours own. The list includes Travelworld, Bridge Travel, Cresta, camping holidays with EuroSites, Tradewinds and Late Escapes (Holiday Auctions Online).

British Airways on Holiday
www.britishairways.com/holiday/ukhols
This site, within the mother British Airways site, is not always easy to find. Click on the wrong button and you will find yourself winging away on European flight bookings. The site takes forever to load but the information, when you finally reach your chosen destination, is excellent. But no online booking.

Brochure Bank
www.brochurebank
This site lets you order up to five brochures from UK-based travel companies.

Disney
www.disney.co.uk
Click on Disneyland Paris or Themeparks USA from the homepage, for details of the Disney holidays and Disney Cruise

Line. You can take a virtual tour around the parks, check out the itineraries and events and buy tickets, or the complete holiday package (see also p.135).

Elegant Resorts International
www.elegantresorts.com

Elegant Resorts originates from Elegant Resorts of Jamaica and offers competitive packages for luxury accommodation in Jamaica, Haiti and Austria. Reservation requests are available online, but confirmation comes later by email or telephone (see also p.139).

Island Outpost
www.islandoutpost.com

A perfect site for those seeking boutique hotels in Miami, Jamaica or the Bahamas (see also p.140).

Page and Moy
www.page-moy.co.uk

This well-respected travel company offers specialist travel, individual or escorted, which take in motor racing, the arts, gardening, opera and music tours.

Powder Byrne
www.powderbyrne.co.uk

This easy-to-use site offers information on PowderByrne's up-market ski holidays for families. There is also an interesting section for corporate groups. Enquiries can be made by email although, like many tour operators, bookings cannot be made online. The site will also offer a ski portal in the near future, with the best ski information on the web, including ski maps, weather, snow quality reports and local information.

Scott Dunn

www.scottdunn.com

This attractive site provides a wealth of information on their world-wide sun and ski holidays, all with a personal touch. The images are terrific, and will have you reaching for the telephone to make a booking before you can say Seychelles. If you are looking for a resort that is special, look here, as everything that is on offer is well-researched.

Travel Choice

www.travelchoice.co.uk

This ABTA-registered tour operator has nearly 30 years of experience in the travel industry, providing holidays and flights to suit all needs. The site is a little light on information and would benefit from more pictures. Curiously, secure online booking is only available during call centre hours.

Auctioneers

The internet auction is one of the success stories of the web world, proving it to be the ideal interactive marketplace to shift unwanted tickets and holidays. It results in far wider participation, leading to more competitive bidding and truer prices.

A flexible travel schedule is necessary to benefit fully from these bargains and it is wise to check out terms and conditions before joining the fray.

The reverse auction is the unique creation of the internet. The concept was pioneered by TravelBids, which is now no longer functional, proving the transitory nature of the internet. The idea caught on and a few sites offer reverse auctions. Bear in mind that there is a fine line between a true reverse auction site and a quotation or tendering service.

www.ebay.co.uk
Ebay

This fun site is not what you would expect an online auction house to be. It almost feels like you are taking part in a game, albeit a simple one, and it is obviously catching on as there are more than 30 million registered users worldwide.

Worried about security? Rest assured, E-bay take fraud very seriously and do their utmost to protect their customers.

You can browse, but if you want to sell or buy you will need to register. Individuals and companies are able to participate in the selling of unwanted stock. New Users will take you through this process, which is lengthy. To zero in on travel items, run down the Categories list on the homepage and click on Tickets and Travel. Alternatively, search using Browse by Themes or use the Search button at the top of the homepage.

Only the seller incurs a listing and final value fee, but this is worth it if you need to offload unwanted tickets of your own, due to unforseen cancellation.

SPECIAL FEATURES

Travel encompasses airlines, bed and breakfast, villas, ferries, cruises, and all kinds of holidays and short breaks. (That's not all however, you can buy and sell virtually anything from this site). The number in brackets after each heading refers to the

overall rating:
★ ★ ★ ★ ★

classification:
auctioneers

updated:
hourly

navigation:
★ ★ ★ ★ ★

content:
★ ★ ★ ★ ★

readability:
★ ★ ★ ★

speed:
★ ★ ★ ★ ★

UK   R

number of items on a particular page. There is not too much on offer, which means checking in to see what is around, but it is possible to find some real bargains, such as two return Eurostar tickets to Paris.

If you are a bargain hunter, then check in from time to time to see what's on offer.

www.lateescapes.com
Late Escapes

overall rating:	★ ★ ★ ★
classification:	auctioneers
updated:	daily
navigation:	★ ★ ★ ★ ★
content:	★ ★ ★
readability:	★ ★ ★ ★ ★
speed:	★ ★ ★ ★ ★

UK   R   at

Late Escapes is part of the Airtours group of companies and aims to become the biggest holiday auction site in the UK. All air holidays and flights have the benefit of being ATOL protected. At the time of review, there were 386 lots available on the site, all from the Airtours stable, but this number fluctuates. A visit a few days later brought up 742 lots.

The site is easy to navigate but you will not pick up the bargains that you might find on other sites. It is difficult to see where you are getting a good deal and perhaps Late Escapes are just using this method of bidding as a marketing tool. After all, it is quite fun waiting to see if you have been successful.

The lots are well described with the status, as in the time remaining in which to bid, clearly shown on the left of the page.

No crazy deals.

overall rating:
★ ★ ★ ★
classification:
auctioneers
updated:
hourly
navigation:
★ ★ ★ ★ ★
content:
★ ★ ★ ★
readability:
★ ★ ★ ★ ★
speed:
★ ★
US

www.priceline.co.uk
Priceline

This reverse-auction site allows you to specify the amount you are willing to pay for flights, hotel rooms and car hire. Priceline will then match this up with suppliers who are prepared to meet these terms. Muddled already? It is a popular formula. Since the company's launch in 1998, they have sold 7.5 million airline tickets and 2.5 million nights of hotel accommodation.

Buyers do not need to register. Simply file your requirements, the amount you are prepared to pay, and provide your credit card number. Priceline will then run a search and if one of the contributors agrees to match your terms, they will purchase the tickets and charge your credit card. This sounds a bit scary and there is no come back once the deal has been struck.

A disadvantage of this site is the inability to have an idle browse. You need to know what you are after.

www.qxl.com
QXL

This pan-European auction site offers consumer-to-consumer and business-to-consumer auctions across Europe. It works by making deals with companies (and individuals) for their slow-moving stock, from an enormous list of categories. Lots of items have no reserve price, which means that you can sometimes pick up a real bargain. Auctions for flight tickets on this site usually last for 24 hours, and after logging a bid (a twenty-second deal) you wait and watch as other bids come in on the page. If a bid is successful, QXL and the seller will email at the close of auction to confirm details. You are also given the opportunity to re-enter the race if you've been outbid in an ongoing auction.

For all travel-related items, click on Travel and Tickets in the Categories bar on the homepage.

Only the seller incurs a Success Fee.

SPECIAL FEATURES

New User walks you through the whole buying and selling process.

Buy Now allows you to buy a holiday through a major tour operator there and then, rather than fight it out in an auction.

overall rating:
★ ★ ★ ★ ★

classification:
auctioneers

updated:
realtime

navigation:
★ ★ ★ ★ ★

content:
★ ★ ★

readability:
★ ★ ★ ★

speed:
★ ★ ★ ★ ★

UK R

You will pay a little more and you have 48 hours to confirm your booking or it will be cancelled. However, fees will be charged.

Weekly alerts is an email service, whereby you receive news of bargains from QXLs most popular categories.

Some bargains to be had, if you log on at the right time.

OTHER SITES OF INTEREST

Holiday Auctions
www.holidayauctions.net
The site name is slightly misleading, as they are not themselves an auction site, but will scour the web for you, searching out the bargains. In order to use the site, you must subscribe first, then register your requirements, whether it be for a holiday or for office stationery. Holiday Auctions will then search the web for you, and email the results. You can then book by phone. The site also offers set price holidays at bargain prices.

Last Minute.com
www.lastminute.com
For holidays, flights, and hotels (see p.23).

Air Travel

There is all-out war amongst the airlines to produce cheaper and cheaper flights but you will find that prices quoted vary widely between portals and it is worth shopping around. If you fly a regular route, register your name with a site and you will be informed when prices are low.

It is interesting to note that since the latter part of 2001, the budget airlines such as Easyjet, Go and Ryanair have all seen an increase in passenger numbers.

Some airlines will allow you to pre-book seats but they do not guarantee you will be given what you want.

overall rating: ★ ★ ★ ★	
classification: directory	
updated: realtime	
navigation: ★ ★ ★ ★	
content: ★ ★ ★	
readability: ★ ★ ★ ★	
speed: ★ ★ ★ ★ ★	
US R at ab	

airlines

http://flyaow.com
Airlines of the Web

AOW was the first index of airline sites on the web and now it boasts a full travel service. It offers agency capabilities, such as car and accommodation bookings, as well as cyber fares and air-travel tips.

Enter the site as a Welcome Guest – but you will need to register if you want to buy.

SPECIAL FEATURES

Private Planes (under Tower) links directly to www.AirCharter.com, who will research executive and group air charters in the US.

An American-biased site but it is useful for linking to 500 airlines.

www.britishairways.com
British Airways

British Airway's UK homepage is fairly sober; there are no distractions. Just click on a link and off you go. Look out for their World Offers and if you book online, you receive a rather nominal £5 discount. Information on BA package holidays is available, but only if one is willing to hang around and wait.

The site has improved their search times, but it still appears that speed is not of the essence here.

SPECIAL FEATURES

Executive Club gives members the ability to choose their own seat. It also allows online check-in up to one hour before departure.

Exclusive Airline Fares lists deals for immediate travel, and as time is at a premium, etickets are issued.

For an airline that is a world leader, the site still falls woefully short, but is improving bit by bit.

overall rating:
★ ★ ★ ★

classification:
airline

updated:
realtime

navigation:
★ ★ ★

content:
★ ★ ★

readability:
★ ★ ★ ★

speed:
★ ★ ★ ★

| UK | at | ab | |

overall rating: ★ ★ ★ ★ ★	
classification: airline	
updated: realtime	
navigation: ★ ★ ★ ★ ★	
content: ★ ★ ★ ★ ★	
readability: ★ ★ ★ ★ ★	
speed: ★ ★ ★ ★ ★	
UK at ab	

www.britishmidland.co.uk
British Midland

British Midland's well-laid-out and straightforward site offers information and booking capability for flights on the busiest and most competitive routes in Europe. They now also fly transatlantic to Washington DC and Chicago.

The site has been overhauled and is much easier to read.

SPECIAL FEATURES

Current BMI Specials gives details of offers, all flying to European destinations. Within this page, click on Destination Guide and Lonely Planet will show you what to do and see.

Diamond Club gives a compelling argument for joining British Midland's frequent flyer programme. Once a member, each flight will win you destinations points, which will earn you a free flight. Other benefits include an extra 20kg baggage allowance and exclusive lounge access.

Timetable allows you to download their timetable as a PDF file, which is very useful for frequent users.

A brilliant, easy-to-use site for the European traveller. It might be useful for some other websites to take note of why the British Midland site is so successful.

www.virgin-atlantic.com
Virgin Atlantic

Voted OAG Airline of the Year 2001, Richard Branson's ventures continue to deliver what customers want. The site, as one would expect, is easy to read, navigate and use. It is a little Flash heavy, which slows down loading time, but it is still worth it. The scarlet screen is very bright but your eyes do adjust to it.

The homepage is simplicity in itself with just six categories to choose from: Book now!, This is Virgin Atlantic, Where and when, Frequent flyer, Our services, and Join in.

SPECIAL FEATURES

Book Now will find you the flight you are looking for. When searching for a flight, use the View Calendar to register the date you wish to fly. This seems to speed up the process, as if you don't it might default to the realtime date. It is also possible to check flight arrivals from this category.

Frequent Flyer earns you miles or rewards. It is divided into three levels to best match your travelling habits.

Our Services offers Travel Classes, which gives descriptions of the three classes, Upper Class, Premium Economy and Economy. It also lists the entertainment provided on each flight.

An excellent site.

overall rating:
★ ★ ★ ★ ★

classification:
airline

updated:
realtime

navigation:
★ ★ ★ ★ ★

content:
★ ★ ★ ★ ★

readability:
★ ★ ★ ★

speed:
★ ★ ★ ★

UK   R   at   ab

overall rating: ★ ★ ★ ★ ★	
classification: e-agent	
updated: daily	
navigation: ★ ★ ★ ★	
content: ★ ★ ★ ★ ★	
readability: ★ ★ ★ ★ ★	
speed: ★ ★ ★ ★	
UK at ab	

low cost air travel

www.cheapflights.co.uk
Cheapflights

This site brings together all the special offers and last-minute bargains it can find on the internet, and many more that are from companies with no internet presence. Rated highly by Good Web Guide readers, Cheapflights can find accommodation, car hire and arrange your insurance, all at the click of a button. The site map gives you an idea of the breadth of Cheapflights. Click on Sitemap at the bottom of the left-hand toolbar.

SPECIAL FEATURES

Hot Deals has First/Business Class discounted flights and can find some excellent deals, although some needed updating.

Legroom Report (under Flight Information in Trip Planning) gives you all the statistics you need to know for stretching out your legs on those long-haul flights.

Fly to outer space? Strange but true. Book your seat on the flight of a lifetime.

Email alerts will send you news by category, flights-only or holidays.

A good site with up-to-the-minute information.

ticket finders

www.deckchair.com
Deckchair

Deckchair was founded in 1999 by Bob Geldof and James Page. Their objective was to offer an easy-to-use flight booking service for the independent traveller. This they have achieved and more. With the acquisition of World Travel Holdings last year, they can now offer even more to their customers.

Deckchair boasts that it is the only flight search and booking facility of its kind, enabling the customer to find the desired information in as few clicks as possible. Speed time has been greatly improved upon. The homepage is clear and uncluttered.

SPECIAL FEATURES

Car hire can have a car ready and waiting for you at your destination.

My Deckchair is a service that allows you to see all your past bookings and view your previous searches. Registration is necessary.

Kasbah provides travel information, from guides to hotels and up-to-the-minute intelligence on every major financial and business centre in the world.

This site offers a superior service for online booking.

overall rating:
★ ★ ★ ★ ★

classification:
e-agent

updated:
regularly

navigation:
★ ★ ★ ★ ★

content:
★ ★ ★ ★ ★

readability:
★ ★ ★ ★ ★

speed:
★ ★ ★ ★

UK   R   at   ab   ia

OTHER SITES OF INTEREST

Airmiles – Travel the World
www.airmiles.co.uk

Just as with any club query, you must have the membership number to get anywhere and password too. Once you've passed these obstacles this website is great for account information and booking enquiries. Essential for the frequent traveller.

Buzz
www.buzzaway.com

This low-cost, ticketless airline offers its flights on a pay-as-you-go basis, flying to 18 destinations across Europe, with nine new routes to Europe planned by Summer 2002. All flights are from Stansted. Book online and you will receive your confirmation number by email. Tickets cannot be refunded but if you need to change a flight, it will cost £10 per person.

Dial a Flight
www.dialaflight.com

Flights and more are offered on this site. It is not yet possible to book online but surely that can only be a matter of time. Download time is very slow, which is a major drawback, and the site does need updating more regularly, but the searches are extensive. Business Saver has some good deals.

EasyJet
www.easyjet.com

EasyJet flies to 16 key European destinations from their four bases in Amsterdam, Geneva, Liverpool and London Luton and their routes are increasing all the time. The majority of sales for these budget flights are derived from the internet and the online booking procedure is well-tuned. Arrival times have been improved on and they now hold a better record than rivals, Go. You can also make use of easyRentacar for car hire at your destination. Register for easyJet email updates for news of special offers and promotions.

Go

www.go-fly.com

Go was British Airway's answer to discount air travel but it is now independently owned. The site is functional and simple to use. At the time of review, Go was offering a £10 discount on all return flights booked online. This represents quite a saving when you are talking of fares well under the £100 mark. If you book regularly with Go, opt for Fast Track, which remembers your address details for future bookings. Join Go Mail and you will be sent advance notice of promotions.

Just the Ticket

www.justtheticket.co.uk

Just the Ticket will search the web for better deals on all flights, holidays and car hire. The search facility is fast and seems to come up with the goods. Latest airline deals is updated regularly. If you are planning a trip to Australia and Argentina or Australia and Japan from London, this is the place to look for good deals. Book via email and Just the Ticket will call within an hour to arrange payment.

Ryanair
www.ryanair.com

Ryanair was the first European airline set up specifically to offer low fares on short-haul intra-European routes. Last year they were voted Best Airline Company in Europe. From its humble beginnings, flying between Dublin and London, Ryanair now works more than 45 routes across 11 countries, carrying seven million passengers a year. Online booking is very simple with some unbelievable bargains to be had. If you fly a route regularly or just like travelling, it is worth registering for their Subscriber Offers. There can sometimes be trouble registering using their direct link. If that is the case, send a separate email. Ryanair has been highly recommended by Good Web Guide readers.

Skydeals
www.skydeals.co.uk

Part of the Thomson Group, Skydeals brings together special offers and published prices on chartered and scheduled flights. It is worth checking out the Special Offers. The site is simply arranged, with a reasonably fast search facility but there are probably better sites that offer you more.

United Airlines
www.ual.com

This huge site offers lots more than just flights. Online booking is easy and some of their special deals are only offered on the internet. Frequent United Airline users can earn Mileage Plus bonus miles.

MORE AIRLINES

Aer Lingus
www.flyaerlingus.ie

Aeroflot
www.aeroflot.co.uk

Air Canada
www.aircanada.ca

Air France
www.airfrance.co.uk

Air India
www.airindia.com

Alitalia
www.alitalia.it/eng

All Nippon Airways
http://svc.ana.co.jp/eng/index.html

American Airlines
www.aa.com

Cathay Pacific
www.cathaypacific-air.com

Crossair
www.crossair.com/en/home/index.html

DAT Airlines
www.dat-airlines.com/en/index_en.htm

Delta Airlines
www.delta.com

Emirates Airlines
www.emirates.com

Finnair
www.finnair.co.uk

Iberia
www.iberia.com/iberia_gb/home.jsp

Icelandair
www.icelandair.co.uk

Japan Airlines
www.jal.co.jp/e/index_e.html

KLM
www.klmuk.co.uk

Lufthansa
www.lufthansa.com

Malaysia Airlines
www.malaysiaairlines.com.my

Qantas
www.qantas.com.au/regions/dyn/home/uk

SAS
www.sas.se

Singapore Airlines
www.singaporeair.com

Swissair
www.swissair.com

Thai Airways International
www.thaiair.com

Rail Travel

Train companies seem to be more adept at their web technology than they are at their core business of railroad transport. Most of the sites are highly efficient and beat waiting on the end of a telephone line for information. The sites generally offer schedules, train status check facilities and online ticket purchasing. Just remember to leave sufficient time for your tickets to arrive by post.

united kingdom

overall rating: ★ ★ ★ ★ ★
classification: rail company
updated: realtime
navigation: ★ ★ ★ ★ ★
content: ★ ★ ★ ★ ★
readability: ★ ★ ★ ★ ★
speed: ★ ★ ★ ★ ★
UK

www.gner.co.uk
GNER

Owned by Sea Containers, GNER operates trains on the East Coast Line between London King's Cross and Scotland. The site offers online reservation and ticket purchase.

SPECIAL FEATURES

Timetable allows you to plan your journey to your selected destination.

How's My Train Running enables visitors to check GNER train arrivals and departures. Running on realtime, this train status check facility is one of the most advanced of UK websites.

GNER WAP Service is an experimental service, letting you access the latest news from your mobile phone. GNER are waiting to see the response from their customers.

A one-stop shop for anyone taking the train to the North of England or Scotland.

www.thetrainline.com
The Trainline

This is the site for the UK rail traveller but when accessing it do not forget the prefix 'the', otherwise you will find yourself looking at the promotional site of a rock band. The Trainline gives details of all train times, ticket bookings and seat reservations on trains in mainland UK.

Registration is required for the first-time user. The site, once you have registered, is easy to use – although the search facility could be faster.

SPECIAL FEATURES

Rail News links through to National Rail's site giving news of disruptions on the lines.

The service is useful for long-term journey planning. Remember to bear in mind delivery time of tickets. For best fares, it may be advantageous to visit the sites of individual rail companies.

overall rating: ★ ★ ★ ★	
classification: ticket agent	
updated: realtime	
navigation: ★ ★ ★ ★ ★	
content: ★ ★ ★ ★	
readability: ★ ★ ★ ★ ★	
speed: ★ ★ ★ ★	
UK R	

OTHER SITES OF INTEREST

Unless stated otherwise, all these sites offer online booking.

Gatwick Express

www.gatwickexpress.co.uk

The fastest way from London to Gatwick but sadly no discount for booking online.

Heathrow Express

www.heathrowexpress.co.uk

This sleek site allows you to book your ticket on BAA's Heathrow Express from Paddington. A fast train leaves every fifteen minutes and with online booking, you receive a £3 discount.

Railtrack

www.railtrack.co.uk

Although you are unable to buy tickets online on this site, it does have its uses, providing a timetable for all UK trains. Look here for latest travel news on the tracks.

Stansted Express

www.stanstedexpress.com

Online booking facility for the 42 minute journey from Liverpool Street.

Thames Trains

www.thamestrains.co.uk

No online booking, but you can check price information, timetables and details of engineering works.

Central Trains
www.centraltrains.co.uk

First Great Western
www.great-western-trains.co.uk

Great Eastern Railways
www.ger.co.uk

Midland Main Line
www.midlandmainline.com

Northern Ireland Transport
www.nirailways.co.uk

ScotRail
www.scotrail.co.uk

South West Trains
www.swtrains.co.uk

Virgin Trains
www.virgintrains.com

europe

overall rating: ★ ★ ★ ★ ★
classification: rail company
updated: realtime
navigation: ★ ★ ★ ★ ★
content: ★ ★ ★ ★ ★
readability: ★ ★ ★ ★ ★
speed: ★ ★ ★ ★ ★
UK

www.eurostar.com
Eurostar

Eurostar's site matches its super-efficient service that it runs between Paris, Lille, Brussels, Disneyland and the French Alps. Timetables and booking pages are easily accessed but unfortunately there is no discount for online booking.

SPECIAL FEATURES
Register your address and you will be kept informed of offers.

Frequent Traveller gives rewards to those who travel between Waterloo and Paris. It is possible to enrol online and then benefit from express check-in, late check-out at partner hotels and a reward scheme for free Eurostar tickets.

Ski Train gives travellers the option of two trains direct to the Alps. To find your way to Ski Train, enter Destination and click on Alps.

An impeccable service.

www.raileurope.co.uk
Rail Europe

Rail Europe is the largest distributor of European travel-related products, catering for both the leisure and business traveller. Owned by SNCF, the French National Railway, Rail Europe is best known for the famous Inter-Rail Pass for travel on Continental Europe. You can book your car onto the train from Calais to the South of France with French Motorail.

The site also covers hotel accommodation in France and Britain.

Prices quoted are in sterling but booking is by telephone only.

An excellent site if you are contemplating continental travel.

overall rating:	★ ★ ★ ★ ★
classification:	rail company
updated:	realtime
navigation:	★ ★ ★ ★ ★
content:	★ ★ ★ ★
readability:	★ ★ ★ ★ ★
speed:	★ ★ ★ ★ ★
FR	

OTHER SITES OF INTEREST

Euro Railways
www.eurorailways.com

An American site, which can tell you everything you need to know about travelling in Europe. It is worth taking a look at this before diverting to individual country's railway sites.

Eurotunnel
www.eurotunnel.com

This site is full of information and news of special offers. Online booking attracts a £2 discount but if you are a member of their customer rewards scheme, you receive a ten per cent discount off all published fares.

Rail Connection
www.railconnection.com

This site will consider your travel plans and then recommend the best rail pass for European travel.

united states

www.4trains.com
4Trains

Part of the 4Anything search engine, this busy site is best-suited for those looking for train services in North America, with the emphasis on the US. Use the search button at the top of the homepage.

SPECIAL FEATURES

Passenger and Freight Lines is a series of links to websites of railway companies all over the world.

Travel and Local Links provides information on other local services for travellers. Visit 4maps.com for planning routes for your onward journey, once you alight the train.

The site is great for accessing timetables, and arming yourself with local journey information before you set off.

overall rating:
★ ★ ★ ★ ★

classification:
search engine

updated:
realtime

navigation:
★ ★ ★ ★

content:
★ ★ ★ ★

readability:
★ ★ ★ ★

speed:
★ ★ ★ ★ ★

US

OTHER SITES OF INTEREST

Amtrak
www.amtrak.com
If you are travelling by train in the US, then this is the site for you. You can work out your itinerary and then book your tickets online but you will need to register first.

TrainWeb
www.trainweb.com
This site is heaven for the rail enthusiast, though the focus of the travel information is primarily on the USA and Canada, you can find out about all the latest news from rail websites around the world. Click on the Travel section for information on journey planning, route guides, tourist railways, and schedules.

worldwide

www.seat61.com
The Man in Seat Sixty-One

This site has all the mystery of a Le Carré epic. Who is this mysterious man who always books Seat 61 on the Eurostar and why has he set up a site devoted entirely to world rail travel? The name's Mark Smith and he is passionate about long-distance rail travel. He has travelled the world far and wide and put all his knowledge into this brilliant site. There are no fur-trimmed anoraks here.

If you want to know how to get from London to Moscow, Mark Smith is the man to ask. Train departure times are given, along with how to book your fare. If that isn't enough information, there are photographs, and details of the sort of seat or berth you can expect to find.

SPECIAL FEATURES

Site search is a quick way to access information if you know what you are looking for.

Useful links will put you in touch with all the railway internet sites in the world.

One of the best websites that the Good Web Guide has seen. You might find yourself boarding a train sooner than you think.

overall rating:
★ ★ ★ ★ ★

classification:
information

updated:
regularly

navigation:
★ ★ ★ ★ ★

content:
★ ★ ★ ★ ★

readability:
★ ★ ★ ★ ★

speed:
★ ★ ★ ★ ★

UK

OTHER SITES OF INTEREST

Orient Express Trains and Cruises
www.orient-expresstrains.com
Book online for the most luxurious of train journeys.

Trans-Siberian - The Russian Experience
www.trans-siberian.co.uk
Click on Destinations and get an overview of the journeys organised by this company that specialises in tailor-made holidays.

TravelNotes
www.travelnotes.org/travel/byrail.htm
Part of the extensive travelnotes.org, this site operates as a search engine providing links to hundreds of train sites. Scroll down the Destination toolbar on the left-hand side of the homepage. Click on the required continent. You can then choose your method of transport by clicking on the desired link.

Voyages Jules Verne
www.vjv.co.uk
This company specialises in offering passengers an altogether different holiday experience, one that evokes a bygone era of travel. Their first journey saw the re-opening of the London-Hong Kong overland and to this, they have now added many other exciting travel adventures.

RoadTravel

Without a doubt, the internet has made it much easier to hire cars around the world. Nearly all travel websites offer car rental, whether it be through a travel portal, e-agent or direct with a company that specialises in car rentals.

The value of the internet is that it can shop around for you and find the best deals. The most important thing to remember to do is to read the small print with reference to insurance and mileage penalties.

overall rating: ★ ★ ★ ★ ★	
classification: car rental	
updated: regularly	
navigation: ★ ★ ★ ★ ★	
content: ★ ★ ★ ★ ★	
readability: ★ ★ ★ ★ ★	
speed: ★ ★ ★ ★ ★	
US	

www.avis.co.uk
Avis

A comprehensive site that takes you through the process of renting a car with great ease. The homepage is simply designed with a series of links, from Online Booking to Rental Locations.

Avis have used a combination of pull-down menus and filling in blanks to enable you to get what you want. It is not too arduous and an answer is returned fairly swiftly. Its particular geographical strength is in the US, but it does have a strong global presence.

The real find with Avis' site is the ability to book online rentals where pick-up is at one location and drop-off is at another.

SPECIAL FEATURES

Special Offers advertises a free extra day on weekend rentals or upgrades.

Guide to Renting is aimed at tourists travelling to Britain.

Products & Services tells you how to rent Prestige Cars.

The site is not overwhelming and is very easy to use.

www.hertz.co.uk
Hertz

This is a well-laid-out site in the company's colours of black and yellow. The homepage is fairly busy, advertising more than just car and van hire. It is worth noting that as the site is directed mostly at business users, rates might not be so competitive for individuals.

Hertz runs special internet rates for car hire in the USA, which include unlimited mileage and loss damage waiver.

The process of ordering online combines a series of clicks through to other pages, asking for yet more information. This could all have been put on one page. In order to get a quote, you must give your email address and it seems that you are unable just to browse in order to compare prices. It is possible to drop off the car at a different location from the pick-up.

SPECIAL FEATURES

Special Offers has details of weekend breakaways, and upgrading a car for a European weekend.

Look elsewhere if you are not a business user. There are better deals around.

overall rating:
★ ★ ★ ★

classification:
car rental

updated:
realtime

navigation:
★ ★ ★ ★

content:
★ ★ ★ ★

readability:
★ ★ ★ ★

speed:
★ ★ ★ ★

US

overall rating: ★ ★ ★ ★ ★	

classification:
car rental

updated:
regularly

navigation:
★ ★ ★ ★

content:
★ ★ ★ ★ ★

readability:
★ ★ ★ ★ ★

speed:
★ ★ ★ ★

UK

www.holidayautos.co.uk
Holiday Autos

This car rental broker is geared towards holidaymakers, rather than the business side of the market. They select the best companies and then negotiate the lowest possible rates from them. They are able to offer some good savings. Holiday Autos has access to more than 4,000 locations worldwide.

Prices are fully inclusive and there is a £5 discount for online booking.

SPECIAL FEATURES

Special Offers change frequently and you will be able to pick up further discounts on car hire around the world.

An efficient site and service so it is not surprising that it is used by several of the leading online travel agents. Holiday Autos are so confident of finding the lowest price that if you succeed in finding somewhere even lower, they will match it.

www.rentadeal.com
Rentadeal

For those travellers visiting major European or US cities, this rent-a-car search engine with online car reservation capabilities is a dream. It will get quotes and availability information on up to 13 different websites. The site also claims that visitors can save up to 40 per cent on hire prices.

Use the drop-down destination menu and click to find your destination. Answer a few questions about dates and make of car that you want and the site does the rest. However, you might find it difficult to get back to Rentadeal's homepage. There are no homepage links and if you press the back page button on your toolbar, you do not necessarily return to the previous page.

SPECIAL FEATURES

Other Cities is hidden away at the bottom of the International Cities drop-down menu, and allows searches for many more cities than specified. Don't be put off by the small number of cities shown on the homepage.

This site is good for researching prices, which are all given in dollars. Sadly there is no currency converter (see p.153 www.oanda.com/converter/travel).

| overall rating: |
| ★ ★ ★ ★ |

| classification: |
| car rental |

| updated: |
| realtime |

| navigation: |
| ★ ★ ★ |

| content: |
| ★ ★ ★ ★ |

| readability: |
| ★ ★ ★ ★ |

| speed: |
| ★ ★ ★ ★ ★ |

| US |

overall rating: ★ ★ ★ ★ ★	
classification: car rental	
updated: regularly	
navigation: ★ ★ ★ ★ ★	
content: ★ ★ ★ ★ ★	
readability: ★ ★ ★ ★ ★	
speed: ★ ★ ★ ★ ★	
US	

www.thrifty.co.uk
Thrifty Car Rental

This refined site is a joy to use, offering instant online quotations for both UK and worldwide car hire. Some overseas locations do, however, require a credit card number before they quote. The system is quick and easy to follow.

You have an option to hire child seats when making a reservation. When answering the question of the driver's age, there is a pull-down menu for you to select an age, from 21 to 70. It would be so much quicker just to type it in.

SPECIAL FEATURES

Sterling Saver Programme is used for overseas rental. Pre-pay for your car hire in the UK in sterling and Thrifty will provide you with a voucher to present upon pick-up of your vehicle.

Latest Promotions gives details of special offers and Lucky Dip at Thrifty Branches. Book a car at a competitive rate, without specifying the make and level. When you turn up on the day, it could be anything from a Ford Ka 1.0L to a Vauxhall Vectra 2.2L.

A site that is purely for the benefit of the UK market but providing a service in 55 countries.

OTHER SITES OF INTEREST

Autoeurope
www.autoeurope.com
This site promises to link you to the best deals for world-wide car rental, along with flights and hotels. They can find you luxury motors to spin around town, all at a price. Compare with other companies beofre booking.

Burgundy Global
www.burgundyglobal.com
This site offers quality world-wide land travel solutions. If you need a people carrier in Rome, a limousine in London, or 50 coaches in Paris, Burgundy Global will sort it out for you.

Budget
www.drivebudget.com
This car hire group offers rental in 3,000 locations around the world. The site has, however, a very American bias towards to it. Only US residents can book online.

Easyrentacar
www.easyrentacar.com
The continuing success of EasyEverything encompasses car rental with the Mercedes A-Class, which can be hired from 14 sites in Europe with further expansion this year. Prices are quoted on a daily basis and you will pay more for weekends. Do read the small print very carefully. Any damage, however small, will be liable to the driver who will have to pay costs up to the excess. If you need to rent a car on spec, you will have to call them.

GoByCoach.com
www.gobycoach.com
This site offers travel information on fares and timetables for buses in the UK and Europe. It also links to information on shuttle services to all UK airports. National Express are strongly encouraging their customers to book online and reward each booking over £5 with Argos Premier Points.

Greyhound Lines
www.greyhound.com
This is the site for that ultimate journey across America in a Greyhound bus. Online booking facility is only for US users.

Boats

Another joy of the worldwide web. Now you can access information on ferry schedules from all around the world. The following sites can provide information on ferries, cruise lines and the waterways of the UK and Europe. You can even reserve online and receive tickets by snail mail for European ferry travel.

overall rating: ★ ★ ★ ★ ★	

overall rating:
★ ★ ★ ★ ★

classification:
e-agent

updated:
regularly

navigation:
★ ★ ★ ★ ★

content:
★ ★ ★ ★ ★

readability:
★ ★ ★ ★ ★

speed:
★ ★ ★ ★ ★

UK   at   ia

ferries

www.ferrybooker.com
Ferrybooker

Launched at the beginning of last year, Ferrybooker.com is the UK's largest online ferry and cross-Channel booking service. This ordered site offers timetables, short breaks, accommodation, car hire, and travel guides, along with online booking for many of the major operators.

To search for timetables and fare prices, use the Book Online tool bar on the left-hand side of the homepage. It couldn't be simpler. You might be able to find more competitive prices by visiting the service provider's own site. They do not always specify the exact fare price but you can always email them.

If you are working out an itinerary, this is the site to visit.

www.ferrytravel.de
Ferry Companies of the World

This site, with delightful sound effects (a ship's horn bellows as you enter the homepage), demonstrates with great panache the glory and usefulness of the web. A directory links to the official websites of ferry companies across the globe, from sailing across the English Channel to Greek island hopping.

Navigation is simple. The homepage presents a list of eight regions in the world, and from there you are presented with a list of ferry companies of the area. Most regions offer quite lengthy lists, with South America being the shortest. This just indicates Latin America's state of doing business on the web versus any failure of the site. Do bear in mind, though, that not all ferry companies have an online presence.

A definite must for a ferry-seeker.

overall rating:
★ ★ ★ ★ ★

classification:
directory

updated:
quarterly

navigation:
★ ★ ★ ★ ★

content:
★ ★ ★ ★ ★

readability:
★ ★ ★ ★ ★

speed:
★ ★ ★ ★ ★

GER

OTHER SITES OF INTEREST

Brittany Ferries
www.brittany-ferries.com
Online booking for ferries from Portsmouth, Poole and Plymouth to France, Ireland and Spain.

Eurodrive
www.eurodrive.co.uk
A simple site that is dedicated to finding and booking the cheapest fares across the English Channel. You can improve on the quoted fares by changing the travel times in the coded boxes. These specify low to peak prices. However, a degree of flexibility on travelling time is needed as Eurodrive cannot necessarily guarantee a booking at the desired time.

Ferrysavers
www.ferrysavers.com
This company will find you the cheapest fare on a number of crossings on ferries in Europe. Input your details and you will be given several options. Needless to say, cheap travel is available at unsociable hours. You have been warned.

P&O Ferries
www.poferries.com
An easily navigable site with an online booking facility but surprisingly little to browse at. It will just search for what you require.

Seafrance Online
www.seafrance.com
Online booking for ferries with savings from Dover to Calais.

Stena Line
www.stenaline.co.uk
Online booking for services between the UK, Ireland and Holland, with a link through to a company specialising in car imports.

Wight Link
www.wightlink.co.uk
Online booking for ferries to and from the Isle of Wight.

overall rating:
★ ★ ★ ★ ★

classification:
information

updated:
frequently

navigation:
★ ★ ★ ★ ★

content:
★ ★ ★ ★

readability:
★ ★ ★ ★

speed:
★ ★ ★ ★ ★

US

cruises

www.cruise.com
Cruise.com

A huge and busy site that caters primarily towards the very popular US cruise market. Cruise.com aims to cut cruise lines' rates by five to ten percent the first time you book. This is an interesting site for those wishing to sail from a US port.

Through a series of steps, the search engine will whittle down the choice available to you until you have exactly what you want. Online booking is not available to non-US residents.

SPECIAL FEATURES

Travel Links provides access to related sites, in particular Cruise Lines. This is probably the most useful tool of the site for UK users.

A well-organised site that is easy to use, especially for gathering information.

www.cruiseinformationservice.co.uk
Cruise Information Service

This well-designed site is part of the Passenger Shipping Association, which represents the world's leading cruise lines. The Cruise Information Service is a source of information for holidaymakers interested in cruising, giving details on types of ships and where cruise lines visit.

The site is tailored towards the individual as well as trade and conference travel. The homepage offers five choices through a series of portholes: Ocean, River/Coastal Cruising, Newsroom, Travel Trade, and Conference & Incentive.

SPECIAL FEATURES

Fact Sheets helps you to decide which cruise is most suited to your requirements.

Free Cruise Booklet is the web version of their printed magazine Choose to Cruise.

Cruise-zine allows you to be kept informed of all that is happening in the cruising world.

The first place you should look if you are thinking about cruising. The site purrs with efficiency.

overall rating:	★ ★ ★ ★ ★
classification:	information
updated:	regularly
navigation:	★ ★ ★ ★ ★
content:	★ ★ ★ ★ ★
readability:	★ ★ ★ ★ ★
speed:	★ ★ ★ ★ ★
UK	

overall rating: ★ ★ ★ ★ ★	# www.cruise2.com
classification: information	Cruise2

overall rating:
★ ★ ★ ★ ★

classification:
information

updated:
realtime

navigation:
★ ★ ★ ★ ★

content:
★ ★ ★ ★ ★

readability:
★ ★ ★ ★

speed:
★ ★ ★ ★

US

www.cruise2.com
Cruise2

This huge non-profit making site is a portal for all information on cruises. The company accepts no paid advertising, has no interest in any travel agency or cruise line and receives no compensation in any form from any participants on the site.

Despite the number of links on the homepage, they are simple to follow. The writing, however, is not particularly easy on the eye and if you choose to scroll down the Alphabetical Site Menu on the left-hand side of the homepage, you will need a magnifying glass.

The site serves travellers, agents and cruise lines with links catering to all three.

SPECIAL FEATURES

Cruise Finder offers an enormous database, which can be searched in several ways.

Top Ten Ships (under Cruise Ships) lists the most popular ships, as selected by cruise newsletters and publications, by a number of categories. Categories include Best Value for Price, Best for Families, and Best Accommodation.

A comprehensive site providing high-quality information.

www.ecruise.co.uk
Ecruise

This site is geared towards the UK user and acts as a cruise portal, covering cruises worldwide from Alaska to Asia.

Search for a cruise by date, duration, budget, destination, cruise line or specific ship. You can also find information by choosing Cruiselines on the left-hand side of the homepage and clicking on categories, from Deluxe down to Standard.

SPECIAL FEATURES

Latest offers will give you access to the best deals around (more than 600 when reviewed), all quoted in sterling. Telephone booking only.

Ship details allows you to find out more details on specific ships and the amenities on offer.

A useful site geared towards the British market.

| overall rating: |
| ★ ★ ★ ★ ★ |

| classification: |
| information |

| updated: |
| daily |

| navigation: |
| ★ ★ ★ ★ ★ |

| content: |
| ★ ★ ★ ★ ★ |

| readability: |
| ★ ★ ★ ★ |

| speed: |
| ★ ★ ★ ★ ★ |

| UK | at | ab | ia |

OTHER SITES OF INTEREST

Classical Cruises
www.classicalcruises.com
Established thirty years ago, Classical Cruises specialises in small-ship cruising on journeys that follow in the footsteps of Odysseus, Charles Darwin and Jason and the Argonauts. This is travel in the luxurious bracket.

CruiseOpinion.com
www.cruiseopinion.com
Database site containing 3,500 cruise reviews, submitted by hardened seafarers. Useful resource if you want honest reviews.

Cunard Line
www.cunardline.com
An attractive homepage beckons would-be cruisers aboard classic ocean cruisers. Read about the history of Cunard Cruising, as well as viewing their destination list and itineraries.

Hebridean Cruises
www.hebridean.co.uk
Cruising in style off the coasts of Scotland and Ireland.

Swan Hellenic
www.swanhellenic.com
The arts and culture feature strongly on these upmarket cruises around Europe, (the Baltic and the Meditteranean), Middle East, Far East and South America. Choose from Ocean, Clipper or river cruises.

TravelPage.com
www.travelpage.com/cruise
Extensive list of ship profiles, cruise reviews and latest news.

www.whatcruise.co.uk
What Cruise?
If you dream of sailing into the sunset, start here by reading the articles from What Cruise? magazine. Register for email alerts for news of bargains.

Youra.com e.guides
www.youra.com/ferry
An American guide to local and international ferry services for a selected number of countries. Good for route planning in countries where the waterways form an integral part of the public transport system.

Freesun
www.freesun.be/cruises.html

P&O Cruises
www.pocruises.com

Princess Cruises and Tours
www.princess.com

travel on the waterways

British Waterways
www.british-waterways.org
This site has information on Britain's waterways and provides links to boat companies where you can rent barges and soak up the atmosphere of this forgotten form of transport.

Drifters
www.drifters.co.uk
Canal holidays portal that links to barge rental companies in England and Wales.

Latelink Boating Holidays
www.latelink.com
This simply designed site offers last-minute boating holidays in the UK and France. Use the search button to find what boats they have available or browse the site by clicking on the flags on the homepage. Email or telephone with your booking details. No online facilities. There are also links to the sister site, www.latelink.cottages.co.uk

Accommodation

When booking a holiday or a business trip, the sites listed in this chapter will help to ensure that your accommodation offers everything that you might want. You can easily narrow down your search to within an inch of your requirements. Find that perfect bolthole in the country, or head for the bright lights and live it up in the city.

hotels

overall rating:	★ ★ ★ ★
classification:	guide
updated:	annually
navigation:	★ ★ ★ ★
content:	★ ★ ★ ★
readability:	★ ★ ★ ★
speed:	★ ★ ★ ★
UK	

www.theaa.com/hotels
AA Hotel Guide

An easy-to-use guide to regional hotels in the UK and Ireland, which forms just part of the AA Guide to Britain. Search by brand or consortium as well as location. The site is informative about places to stay, even in the remotest parts of the UK, and has just introduced online booking for many of the hotels on its database. For these, you can check availability and will receive instant booking confirmation.

The AA can be forgiven for the rather uninspiring design of the homepage, since what it lacks in aesthetic appeal it more than makes up for in the amount and quality of information on offer.

To find a hotel, use the Interactive Map or type a location in the blank box on the left-hand side of the homepage. Register your requirements from the drop-down menus. You can also link to AA Premier Hotels, Hotel Groups and Consortia and Special Hotel Offers by clicking on the logos.

We have had some trouble linking straight through to the hotels page. If the link is not working then try the AA's main homepage at www.theaa.com, and click on Hotels under Find, in the left-hand toolbar.

SPECIAL FEATURES

Where to Stay gives you a map of the area with the choices available to you and a list, with links, detailing the type of accommodation and food quality.

Where to Eat provides a somewhat limited list of restaurants and eateries, with a strong English and French bias.

The site provides a good source of information.

overall rating: ★ ★ ★ ★	# www.accomodata.com AccomoData
classification: search engine	The name of this site is slightly misleading in that it offers much more than just accommodation; search also for flights, car rental and travel information.
updated: daily	
navigation: ★ ★ ★ ★	To get straight to the accommodation search, click on the logo in the centre of the homepage to find a destination index that encompasses the world. The links for each destination are impressive. For the UK, you will be presented with the choice of hotels, bed and breakfasts and self-catering rentals, the latter including canal boats and caravans.
content: ★ ★ ★ ★ ★	
readability: ★ ★ ★ ★	
speed: ★ ★ ★ ★	*This is not the most attractive of sites but it is full of information.*
UK	

www.ase.net
Accommodation Search Engine Network

This search engine lists more than 200,000 accommodation web pages from all over the world. Browse the site by using the search facility at the top of the homepage or click on the Destination links.

The search facility is fairly slow but does come up with the goods. Online booking is applicable in some cases.

SPECIAL FEATURES

Languages can be found at the top of the homepage and enables you to set the room rates in the currency of your choice.

Preferences allows you to set your requirements, so that the search engine will automatically default to them, when you are looking for accomodation.

The design of this site is outmoded and disappointing. Do not be put off by this as the site definitely has its uses.

overall rating: ★ ★ ★ ★
classification: search engine
updated: frequently
navigation: ★ ★ ★ ★ ★
content: ★ ★ ★ ★
readability: ★ ★ ★
speed: ★ ★ ★
US

overall rating:	
★ ★ ★ ★ ★	
classification:	
search engine	
updated:	
regularly	
navigation:	
★ ★ ★ ★ ★	
content:	
★ ★ ★ ★ ★	
readability:	
★ ★ ★ ★ ★	
speed:	
★ ★ ★ ★ ★	
UK	

www.cheapnights.com
Cheap Nights

Cheap Nights is the sister of Cheap Flights (see p.66, air travel section) and as such provides an information and booking service for accommodation worldwide. They cover more than 200 destinations, each with its own dedicated page. UK destinations are limited to major cities only.

To start your search, choose the first letter of your destination from the A to Z tool bar at the top of each page. Click on the city and you will be presented with a series of choices and links to the best deals in town.

SPECIAL FEATURES

Links on the destination pages gives you useful information on the city, the weather, a printable currency comparison chart and more.

Rough Guides reviews the accommodation in association with Cheapnights and this is the only site where you can find these listings and book online.

A useful site for booking rooms worldwide.

www.hotelguide.com
Hotel Guide

This Swiss-owned site is one of the largest online hotel directory, where you can find hotels and link to their online booking services. The site has an exceptionally large and comprehensive listing, although many are in the luxury bracket. It is best to stick to the cities listed. Attempts to find hotels in more remote parts were unsuccessful.

SPECIAL FEATURES

Mobile Internet allows you to search the directory from your mobile phone, using WAP.

Currency Converter enables you to calculate hotel rates into your chosen currency.

Clock enables you to check out the time around the world.

A slick site if you are looking for something with that bit extra.

overall rating:
★ ★ ★ ★ ★

classification:
directory

updated:
realtime

navigation:
★ ★ ★ ★ ★

content:
★ ★ ★ ★ ★

readability:
★ ★ ★ ★ ★

speed:
★ ★ ★ ★ ★

SW

| overall rating: |
| ★ ★ ★ ★ |

| classification: |
| e-agent |

| updated: |
| realtime |

| navigation: |
| ★ ★ ★ ★ |

| content: |
| ★ ★ ★ |

| readability: |
| ★ ★ ★ ★ |

| speed: |
| ★ ★ ★ ★ |

| US | |

www.hotelstravel.com
HotelsTravel

HotelsTravel is a misleading name for what is essentially a full online travel agent giving links to 75,000 lodging and travel-related resources worldwide. To get the best use out of this site, click on Hotels and Travel Destinations. Unfortunately, you are several clicks away from finding out exactly what you want. When the information is served up, though, it's pretty good.

The site provides no 'About Us' on the homepage. This has become fairly standard practice for websites. Instead it invites businesses to add to their site for a one off fee. If you choose to book a room through this site, it may be worth checking out the hotel's credentials elsewhere.

Despite a strong American bias, this site is a good starting point for research.

www.laterooms.com
LateRooms

LateRooms is a new concept for hotels. Hotels contact LateRooms with their late availability bedrooms and then customers visiting the site can take advantage of the savings on offer. After all, an occupied room, at whatever low rate, is better than an empty one.

LateRooms is not the most exciting of all sites but it is easy to use. Search by entering a town or region, fill in a few details and, hey presto, the results will come flashing up. At first glance it is unclear which countries are covered, but clicking on More, reveals all the information you need.

Sadly, online booking is not a feature of this site at the moment. Telephone the hotel direct, mentioning LateRooms, and pay by credit card.

SPECIAL FEATURES

Change country or language in the top right-hand corner of the homepage allows you to view hotels and holiday rentals in a number of countries.

This site is very worthwhile, despite its utilitarian looks. Visit the sister site at www.latelet.com if you are looking for a villa or a house to rent, and www.latecabins.com for berths on cruises (UK departures only).

overall rating:	★ ★ ★ ★ ★
classification:	search engine
updated:	realtime
navigation:	★ ★ ★ ★
content:	★ ★ ★ ★ ★
readability:	★ ★ ★
speed:	★ ★ ★ ★
UK	

overall rating: ★ ★ ★ ★ ★	
classification: guide	
updated: occasionally	
navigation: ★ ★ ★ ★ ★	
content: ★ ★ ★ ★	
readability: ★ ★ ★ ★ ★	
speed: ★ ★ ★ ★ ★	
UK	

www.wolsey-lodges.co.uk
Wolsey Lodges

Wolsey Lodges are more than bed and breakfasts: they are private homes where guests are made welcome as friends. Founded in 1981, the lodges can provide hospitality in some of Britain's most prestigious locations. There are a few Wolsey Lodges in France, Italy and Spain, mostly run by ex-pats. Accommodation varies from grand country houses with antiques to more modest homes.

The site looks a little outdated but all the information is there, along with some good pictures of houses and bedrooms. There are some email links for bookings.

SPECIAL FEATURES

Find out more tells you what to expect when staying at a Wolsey Lodge. Search by region and you will find that the UK is fairly well covered. Each entry links to a map so you know exactly where you are heading for.

This is an excellent concept. Standards are very high and you can rest assured that you will find a warm welcome. If you are unwilling to fork out hotel rates then the places offered on this site might fit the bill.

www.leisurehunt.com
LeisureHunt

This site is aimed at travellers in the UK, providing information on hotels, bed and breakfasts, campsites, hostels and self-catering apartments and cottages. The site is easily navigable, with six choices on the homepage: UK Accommodation, Worldwide Accommodation, UK Top Cities, UK Airport Hotels, and Top World Cities (this has a huge database, drawing from 69,000 properties).

Coverage of the UK seems to be the most in-depth, with spot-on results for even the most out-of-the-way locations. The foreign searches yielded less quality for rural and suburban destinations but more than enough for city requests.

A swift and wide-ranging accommodation booking service with listings to suit every wallet.

| overall rating: |
| ★ ★ ★ ★ |
| **classification:** |
| directory |
| **updated:** |
| regularly |
| **navigation:** |
| ★ ★ ★ ★ |
| **content:** |
| ★ ★ ★ ★ |
| **readability:** |
| ★ ★ ★ ★ ★ |
| **speed:** |
| ★ ★ ★ ★ ★ |
| UK |

OTHER SITES OF INTEREST

Country House Hotels
www.country-house-hotels.com
This simple black-and-white site divides the country house hotels guide into eleven regions around Great Britain. The database is not that extensive although the majority of the hotels are in historic houses. To book, you must either telephone or email your requirements.

Hotelnet
www.hotelnet.co.uk
This company features global hotel chains and consortia, as well as some independent hotels. Prices seem fairly uncompetitive, but click on to Special Offers, and you will find some bargains.

villas

www.1001-villa-holidaylets.com
1001 Holiday Villas

It is difficult to know where to start when faced with such an overcrowded homepage. The site is clearly laden with information about villas worldwide. If you know your chosen destination, then the process of finding a suitable property is not difficult. Properties are rented directly from owners.

There are numerous ways to search for a villa: by keyword, by country or by world region. The Quick Search facility on the left-hand side of the homepage features topics such as Top Golf, Top Skiing and Search by Price. The details provided are comprehensive and the photographs good.

SPECIAL FEATURES

Hot Property gives details of one of the best properties the site has to offer.

Latest Property allows visitors to view properties that have just come on to the letting market.

The site has a lot to offer – though not online booking, as that is done direct with the owners, but you can send an email to get the ball rolling.

overall rating:	★★★★★
classification:	directory
updated:	regularly
navigation:	★★★★★
content:	★★★★★
readability:	★★★★
speed:	★★★★★
UK	

overall rating:	
classification: search engine	
updated: regularly	
navigation:	
content:	
readability: ★ ★ ★ ★ ★	
speed: ★ ★ ★ ★	
UK	

www.holidayleaders.com
Holiday Leaders

Holiday Leaders acts independently to find your ideal holiday rental. The site offers one of the largest property portfolios in the world and is compiled from a collection of quality, owner-managed homes and also those managed by the leading rental companies.

The refined search engine is simple to manage, and within a few clicks you will have a number of properties ready to view.

SPECIAL FEATURES

N for navigation is a logo found on each page on the right-hand side. Click it and up will come a small window, enabling you to get around the site.

Suitcase enables you to add properties to a shortlist so that you can compare prices. Registration is necessary to use this facility.

Good worldwide selection of top-of-the-range villas and apartments.

www.holiday-rentals.com
Holiday Rentals

This busy site offers more than 6,000 rentals worldwide. From the homepage, you can search for properties by destination or activity (restricted to just golf and skiing). If you need to be nudged gently in the right direction, click on Holiday Ideas and you can choose between villas with pools, city accommodation, and even yachts. The design of the homepage is not overly appealing but the contents certainly are.

Booking is with the owners direct and therefore not online.

Holiday-rentals can also book your flights, car hire, and insurance through their partners.

SPECIAL FEATURES

About Us gives details of the workforce at Holiday-Rentals, with particular emphasis given to their Director and Deputy Director of Greetings (DOGS).

Choice Properties is a selection of the finest properties for hire. Look for the wedding cake villa in Cannes at £9,200 a week.

A site worth looking at.

overall rating:
★ ★ ★ ★ ★

classification:
directory

updated:
frequently

navigation:
★ ★ ★ ★ ★

content:
★ ★ ★ ★ ★

readability:
★ ★ ★ ★

speed:
★ ★ ★ ★

UK

overall rating: ★ ★ ★ ★	
classification: search engine	
updated: infrequently	
navigation: ★ ★ ★ ★ ★	
content: ★ ★ ★ ★	
readability: ★ ★ ★ ★	
speed: ★ ★ ★	
UK	

www.privatevillas.co.uk
Private Villas

This site puts visitors in touch with villa owners and small companies offering villa accommodation. Choose from various locations in the world and then make several selections, allowing the search engine to gear into action. For further information, contact details of the owner/company are given and booking must be made direct through them.

The site can also organise flights, car hire, insurance and holiday loans through the AA.

SPECIAL FEATURES

Index lists countries and specific locations, where you can hope to find the villa of your dreams.

The spinning globe on the homepage is a little off-putting but you might just find what you are looking for.

www.villaclick.com
Villaclick

This site, with playschool graphics, is a simple one to navigate. Villaclick.com has 591 villas and apartments (in Portugal, Spain and Florida) on its books. The search facility is child's play and the results produce good photographs and details of the villas. All villas can be booked online with major credit cards.

Flights and car hire can be arranged through Villaclick.

SPECIAL FEATURES

My Villas will save and store details of properties and even email them to friends.

The site is not overwhelming and you are not confronted by a mass of information. In fact, it is really rather good.

overall rating:
★★★★★

classification:
e-agent

updated:
regularly

navigation:
★★★★★

content:
★★★★★

readability:
★★★★

speed:
★★★★★

UK

OTHER SITES OF INTEREST

Elysian Holidays
www.elysianholidays.co.uk
(see p.41)

French Affair
www.frenchaffair.com
Villas and houses in France.

Holiday Bank
www.holidaybank.co.uk
Although operating as a full agent, one of the best parts of this site is its Holiday Accommodation. You could find some cosy boltholes to hire in some of Europe's most beautiful cities.

Spanish Affair
www.spanishaffair.com
Villas and houses in Spain.

Tuscany Now
www.tuscanynow.com
This company has been specialising in luxury villa and apartment rentals for the past ten years. Of particular interest are the apartments in Florence, Rome and Venice – imagine staying in a palazzo overlooking the Piazza Santa Croce. This must be the way to sample Italy, living life among the locals.

bed and breakfast

www.beduk.co.uk
B&B My Guest

This site allows you to choose from 300 bed-and-breakfast establishments in the UK. Search the country by county name or click a county on the map. The search is on the slow side and the results can sometimes be disappointing.

This is bed and breakfast on a slightly grander scale than you might expect and is aimed at visitors to the UK. The properties are quintessentially British, some with hundreds of years of history but all providing mod cons. You can book online.

SPECIAL FEATURES

ETC Accommodation Ratings explains the English Tourism Council's ratings for bed and breakfasts. It is worth reading this so that you know what to expect.

If you are looking for more than just a bed for the night, then this site can offer that little bit extra – but without your having to fork out hotel rates.

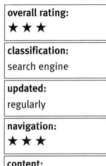

overall rating:
★ ★ ★

classification:
search engine

updated:
regularly

navigation:
★ ★ ★

content:
★ ★ ★ ★

readability:
★ ★ ★

speed:
★ ★ ★

UK

OTHER SITES OF INTEREST

Bed and Breakfast.com
www.bedandbreakfast.com
Founded by a seasoned B & B traveller in 1994, this site covers inns (hotels), and B & Bs world-wide. Now part of worldRes.com, the site has continued to grow, offering unparalled choice in this particular market. To search by country, use the drop-down menu on the homepage, or use the map search. Online booking is available.

Bed and Breakfast for Garden Lovers
www.bbgl.co.uk
This network was established several years ago by keen gardeners, for gardeners. Sue Colquhuon, the organiser, knows all the members personally, and visits each property on her books on a regular basis. All BBGL properties are located in quiet locations and several hosts provide dinner, if required. This is a very worthwhile site to have up your sleeve, if you are looking for a bed for the night.

Bed & Breakfast in Italy
www.bbitalia.com
This gem of a site has some wonderful little bed-and-breakfast establishments, studios and apartments to rent in some of Italy's most beautiful cities and towns. Click on a city and in order to view all the properties, click on the white arrow on the right-hand side of the page. Booking is by credit card only.

cottages and castles

Classic Cottages
www.classiccottages.co.uk
This well-designed site covers cottages in the West Country. It could not be easier to use, with full descriptions and photographs of what's on offer. Search by region or by your requirements, answering a series of drop-down blanks. The search engine is fast and efficient. Mull over the results and add your favourites to your shortlist.

English Country Cottages
www.english-country-cottages.co.uk
This company has over 3000 properties on its books, and now extends to Ireland and France. Each property listed has been checked thoroughly by the company. Online booking is not offered, but you can check the availability of properties.

Landmark Trust
www.landmarktrust.co.uk
Choose from over 160 historic buildings across Britain for your self-catering holiday, and at the same time, you will be saving another historic building from neglect and disrepair. Four houses in Italy and one in Vermont have recently been added to their portfolio.

Latelink Cottages
www.latelink.cottages.co.uk
A useful site for finding cottages at short notice. They have properties in the UK and France, with over 3000 to choose from.

Loyd and Townsend Rose
www.ltr.co.uk
This portfolio of some of Scotland's finest houses, baronial mansions and castles can provide accommodation for personal and corporate use. A small site, but highly selective.

camping and caravans

Camp Sites.co.uk

www.camp-sites.co.uk

This site will find you somewhere in Great Britain to park your caravan, or pitch a tent. The site also stretches to finding hotels.

Keycamp Holidays

www.keycamp.co.uk

This company can offer upmarket, and well-equipped, mobile homes, or their super tent (complete with fitted kitchen), at 120 sites in eight European countries. There are also free Keycamp Children's Clubs on several of their sites. Online booking is not available, but you can email your requirements, and then book by telephone.

Oginet European Camping Index

www.oginet.com/camping

This busy-looking site is an extensive directory of links to camping and caravanning sites across Europe.

hostels

Hostels.com
www.hostels.com

This American site has details of hostels worldwide and 50 are now bookable online, but more will soon be jumping on the information super highway.

Youth Hostels Association
www.yha.org.uk

A surprising number of youth hostels now have online booking. More surprising, perhaps, is the fact that some, in city locations, boast en suite bathrooms. They are not just for youths either; families can join in the fun too.

boutique and luxury hotels

Relais Chateaux
www.relaischateaux.fr
This is an association that unites some of the most prestigious and charming hotels and restaurants in the world. Online reservation is available and you are able to track your reservation and modify your requirements. You can also download the guide by regions in PDF format.

Design Hotels
www.designhotels.com
This site represents some very select establishments with excellent information and pictures on each hotel.

Leading Hotels of the World
www.lhw.com
This is luxury at the top end of the market, but there are some special offers worth looking out for.

Preferred Hotels and Resorts
www.preferredhotels.com
Useful for last minute reservations.

Small Luxury Hotels of the World
www.slh.com
This site is small but perfectly formed, offering 280 hotels worldwide.

Hotel Groups

Banyan Tree Resorts
www.banyantree.com

Hilton Hotels
www.hilton.com

The Lanesborough
www.lanesborough.com

Mandarin Oriental
www.mandarin-oriental.com

Meridien Forte Hotels
www.lemeridien-hotels.com

Orient Express Hotels
www.orient-expresshotels.com

Raffles International
www.raffleshotel.com

Ritz Carlton
www.ritzcarlton.com

The Ritz London
www.theritzhotel.co.uk

The Savoy Group
www.savoy-group.co.uk

Sheraton Hotels
www.sheraton.com

Special Interest Travel

This chapter is dedicated to fulfilling all those pipedreams, whether you are an urban cowboy and want to get a taste of the real thing or fancy a cooking course in Tuscany. The internet is a huge resource for such things and the sites suggested are just a sliver off the icing on the cake.

Nowadays, travellers are demanding more than just a holiday. They are seeking adventure in far off and unusual destinations, and the internet does not let them down. There's a holiday for the adventurous traveller, whatever their taste. If the sites featured here are unable to cater for a specific choice, they can certainly point you in the right direction, or help to plan a trip around individual adventures.

PORTALS

Infohub
www.infohub.com

This site allows you to search for a holiday by activity. Scroll down the seemingly endless list of choices and you have a jumping-off point into the world of discovery.

ADVENTURE

Across the Divide
www.atd-expeditions.co.uk

This company specialise in adventurous but safe holidays; mini-expeditions for the energetic. Events can be tailor-made for fund-raising and promotional purposes. Each tour presents a challenge and at the same time can raise funds for charities. If you are looking for something with that little bit extra, then take a look at this site.

Serioussports
www.serioussports.com
This site is the premier directory for outdoor and adventure sports outfitters based in the Americas. It is not easy to get a company listed here and only the best warrant a full description on the site. Browse sports by Air, Land and Sea but you may find it difficult to find something a little closer to home.

Sherpa Online
www.sherpa-walking-holidays.co.uk
This site encompasses walking and cycling holidays in a variety of destinations worldwide. Search for a holiday using the drop-down boxes, the results of which will bear in mind your preference for difficulty level. This thankfully ranges from easy to expert.

Tall Stories
www.tallstories.co.uk
Tall Stories offers adventure sports holidays in Europe, fulfilling your desire for adrenalin-rushing kicks. Try Hotdogging in a two-man inflatable canoe down rapids. Waht about Canyoning, a sport that takes in abseiling, rock climbing and scrambling over boulders . This site is not for couch potatoes or the faint-hearted.

Wild Dog Adventure Travel
www.wild-dog.com
Use this well-organised site to find tour operators who specialise in wild holidays, offering more than 10,000 different adventure holiday options. The Directory can be used for searching by country or activity. The Perfect Lead is a personalised service whereby Wild Dog does all the legwork for you.

ART HISTORY

Art History Abroad
www.arthistoryabroad.com
Modern Grand Tours of Italy for gap-year students and adult culture vultures.

BARGAIN AND DISCOUNT

If you are looking for value-for-money or a last-minute bargain, the internet provides the ideal medium for travel companies to offer late deals.

Bargain Holidays
www.bargainholidays.com
Specialising in late-availability holidays or flight-only deals from the UK. Choose a budget limit and proceed or use the Quick Holiday Search and see what is available. Telephone bookings only.

Budget Travel
www.budgettravel.com
All you need to know about travelling around the world ... on a budget. Plenty of links to useful sites. People who know what they are talking about have put the site together.

My Price Tracker
www.mypricetracker.com
If you are looking for a last minute bargain, start your search here. Track prices until they come into your price range or list your requirements in advance and Mypricetracker will let you know of any deals. Registration is necessary.

DIVING

Regaldive Worldwide
www.regal-diving.co.uk
This award-winning site offers diving holidays for the novice to the experienced. The majority of holidays take place in the Red Sea, as it is an ideal place to learn to dive and train. Liveaboards give you the opportunity to live right over dive sites and to experience secluded dives that are not available to day-boat divers.

FAMILY

Centerparcs
www.centerparcs.com
Centerparcs operate in England, France, Germany and Holland, each offering similar facilities, set to a high standard. They cater for everyone: grandparents can find peace, Mum can be pampered, Dad can be sporty and the kids can have fun.

Disneyland Paris
www.disneylandparis.com/uk
This site is slow to load but full of the magic that a trip to Disneyland can offer.

Disney's USA Resorts
www.disney.co.uk/usa-resorts
If you are considering a family trip to the USA, why not take in a Disney resort? Get your children to look at the site, they'll love it.

Abercrombie and Kent
www.abercrombiekent.co.uk

The pioneers of luxury holidays to exotic and inaccessible places have now extended their portfolio to include family holidays, for children between five and twelve. They offer a multitude of choices from buckets and spades to adventures in the wild. Their ship, the Explorer, has a number of cruises including Antarctic and Amazonian cruises, providing a great learning experience.

Dragoman
www.dragoman.co.uk

This overland operator can provide family trips of the most adventurous kind in Africa and Peru. Minimum age is eight.

Exodus
www.exodus.co.uk

It is possible to take children (minimum age of five) on some of their adventure holidays, although it is not particularly evident on the site (see p.42).

Esprit Holidays
www.esprit-holidays.co.uk

This company specialises in family holidays in the Alps in both the summer and winter.

Family Travel
www.family-travel.co.uk

Everything you need to know about travelling with children. Registration is necessary and once there is more information on the site, a subscription will be charged. The site promises an extensive database on destinations and types of family holidays.

Travelbag Adventures
www.travelbag-adventures.com
Click on Family Trips and you will find details of sixteen itineraries taking in a wide range of activities from canoeing in the Rockies to elephant spotting in Sri Lanka. Minimum age is five.

FISHING

Go Fishing Worldwide
www.go-fishing-worldwide.com/Go-Fishing-Ww/
This company organises freshwater and saltwater fishing around the world. With a map of the fishing world and the illustrated fishing index, this site is fun to use and is packed with information.

FOOD AND WINE

Tasting Places
www.tastingplaces.com
If you are looking for an upmarket cooking holiday, then let Tasting Places do the job for you. With locations in Greece, Italy and Thailand and some of the world's finest chefs (including Alastair Little and Peter Gordon), this could be your dream holiday. The company goes from strength to strength, rated by Condé Nast Traveller as one of the ten best cookery holidays in the world, and by the Sunday Times as one of the top 100 best holidays.

France in Your Glass
www.inyourglass.com
Vineyard touring holidays in France with internationally recognised authorities on wine.

GENERAL INTEREST

Shaw Guides
www.shawguides.com
This site is huge and packed with information to find 'learning' holidays around the world. The Guide to Recreational Cooking Schools is excellent. Also look here for language vacations, photography, golf and tennis camps, and writer's workshops.

Go Now Travel
www.go-nowtravel.com
This site, which is part of the Page & Moy group, recently won the Daily Telegraph best website award. As a portal, the site can satisfy all your travel needs in a simple and efficient manner. See also Page and Moy (p.52).

GOLF

3DGolf
www.3dgolf.co.uk
3Dgolf specialise in European golfing holidays, although they do offer some US destinations.

LUXURY TRAVEL

For most of us, these holidays remain but a dream – but a very good one.

Abercrombie & Kent
www.abercrombiekent.co.uk
A wonderful site from the pioneers of luxury holidays, specialising in safaris, and the exotic. (see also p.136 for their family holidays).

dreamClick
www.dreamclick.com
Offering some of the coolest and most luxurious leisure opportunities, this site will help you find something special.

Elegant Resorts
www.elegantresorts.co.uk
This site offers various seasonal luxury holidays and is an excellent place to look for the very exclusive and very expensive hotels and resorts.

Elegant Resorts International
www.elegantresortsint.com
This company has put together competitive packages for holidays in Antigua, Jamaica, Mexico and South Africa.

Goodacre & Townsend
www.goodtown.co.uk
This travel consultancy provides a very personal planning service. With their wealth of experience, they can assist you in defining the true meaning of luxury travel.

Grand Trunk
www.grandtrunk.com

This new site is devoted to the pursuit of luxury. Contributors are leading independent travel writers and they have stayed in the hotels that they write about. Where else could you read about Olga Polizzi's favourite restaurants in Rome? A magnificent site that is set to become a leader in the world of luxury travel.

Island Outpost
www.islandoutpost.com

A perfect site for those seeking boutique hotels in Miami, Jamaica or the Bahamas.

Luxury Link
www.luxurylink.com

This red carpet site presents an impressive collection of luxury holidays, resorts, romantic weekends and travel news. Look at the Auction Page – even rich people like to have some fun.

The Mediterranean Experience
www.themed.net

This company specialises in tailor-made holidays of the most luxurious kind. Some of the best hotels in the Mediterranean can be found in their books but also smaller, less well-known ones are given floor space. Bargains you will not find.

Quintessentially
www.quintessentially.com

This is a members only club (£400 p.a.) that can smooth your path through life. They deal with all travel requests, from finding a private jet, to arranging a car to pick you up from the airport.

Membership of this elite club affords you entry to certain London clubs, gyms and reservations at restaurants. The Priority Pass gives access to over 300 VIP lounges at airports worldwide.

OLDER TRAVELLERS

Saga
www.saga.co.uk
This well set out site offers a variety of travel options at reasonable prices. Travel insurance is offered at discount prices. The bad news is that at least one member of your party has to be over 50, and another over 40. So you may just have to wait a while before you can enjoy Saga world.

RANCH HOLIDAYS

Ranchweb
www.ranchweb.com
If you fancy yourself as a cowboy, this site is the world directory. But if the thought of horses makes you shudder, the site extends to spas, golfing and the luxurious.

SAFARI

Safari Link
www.safarilink.com
This excellent search engine connects with what would otherwise be a very fragmented and hard-to-access market. Search by logging in your Dream Safari, or by region.

SAILING

Salty Seas
www.saltyseas.com
This yacht-charter company can find you a dreamboat, whether crewed or self-sail, from its many contacts in the Mediterranean, Caribbean and South Pacific.

SKIING

Alp Leisure
www.alpleisure.com
This company specialise in luxury catered chalets in Méribel, France, which are situated next to the pistes.

Board-it
www.board-it.com
Search for the ultimate boarding experience on this site. Book the holiday, get the gear and find the slopes. It's all here.

Directski
www.directski.com
Founded by two skiing enthusiasts, this company is going from strength to strength. They operate in some of Europe's top ski resorts and offer the full package of apartment and hotel accommodation, and necessary kit to slope away.

IfYouSki
www.ifyouski.com
The site, formerly known as Complete Skier, has plenty to offer, from Best Deals to Quality Chalets. The site is particularly strong

on resort jobs with some of the best operators, giving sound employment advice to hopeful ski youths. Flashmaps, under Pics 'n Fun, lets you zoom in on selected resorts to size up the runs on offer. Check out their sister sites: ifyougolf.com, ifyoudive.com and ifyouexplore.com. This is one-stop shopping, although online booking is not an option...at the moment.

Meriski

www.meriski.co.uk

This company confines its activities to Méribel, France, and its 14 chalets are amongst the village's finest. Offering a team of ten qualified NNEB nannies, MeriKids Club and superlative comfort for adults, Meriski can cater to all your needs. Excellent photographs of all the chalets so you can be sure of what to expect. Telephone bookings only.

Snow Forecast

www.snow-forecast.com

This site is brilliant for finding out snowfalls and forecasts at your intended skiing resort. If you are a regular skier, bookmark it.

Ski Scotland

www.ski-scotland.com

Scotland seems to get forgotten as a potential ski resort and this newly launched site aims to set the record straight. With five areas to choose from, click on piste maps and see what each resort has to offer. The site has information on travel and accommodation.

See also Powder Byrne p.52 (Tour Operators).

SPA

Spas Directory
www.worldhealthspa.com
A fairly direct site, listing Spas in the United Kingdom, along with treatments offered.

Thermalia Travel
www.thermalia.co.uk
This British company specialises in spa holidays and can find locations in Europe, Asia and Africa.

TENNIS HOLIDAYS

Tennis Holidays
www.tennisholidays.co.uk
This specialist site will help you choose the right resort (in Spain or Portugal), which matches all your requirements. Not only confined to tennis, a range of sports is on offer, taking in golf, mountain biking, riding and water sports. You can also book flights, car hire and insurance through the company.

WEEKENDS AND SHORT BREAKS

Inntravel
www.inntravel.co.uk
Inntravel specialise in short breaks in Europe. Choose from walking, cooking, cycling, cross-country skiing, and riding, all throughout Europe. This slick site will help you to narrow down your search and find something perfect.

TravelScene

www.travelscene.co.uk

This company has thirty years of experience in short break holidays. If you have a flight, they can arrange the accommodation. The site is easy to follow, and the recommendations are price conscious.

Web Weekends

www.webweekend.co.uk

This site, the only one dedicated solely to weekend travel, caters for weekenders of all sorts, from family breaks at Alton Towers to culture in Rome. Top Ten Weekends lists their weekly offers.

Miscellaneous

This chapter brings together all the loose ends. Where to check a tour operator's credentials, how to find out about vaccinations, and what to do if it all goes horribly wrong.

CONSUMER PROTECTION

The following are travel bodies that oversee the travel industry. If you have any problems, they should be your first port of call.

Air Travel Organisers' Licence
www.atol.org.uk

ATOL was founded to protect the public from losing their money or being stranded abroad when an air travel company collapses. It aims to give consumer protection to people in the UK who buy flights or air holidays. Visitors can check that a travel firm holds a licence to sell flights and air package holidays. The site's Consumer Information section gives advice on how to handle difficulties experienced with a tour operator and the best way to make a claim or report an unlicensed operator. If you are looking for a refund on a trip that failed to deliver, visit this site first.

Association of British Travel Agents
www.abta.com

This site is ABTA's web directory, which provides users with information on its 2300 UK member companies, and offers information on each travel company's speciality. Search the directory either by destination or special interest. Visitors can order brochures online or use the Infolink to request more details.

International Air Transport Association
www.iata.org

This is the main association for the airline industry. The site provides information to travellers about the validity of airlines. To check out an airline, go to Membership and search by name or geographical area.

CONSUMER RIGHTS

The following sites will help you put together a complaint and ensure that it gets sent to the right person.

Air Transport Users Council

www.auc.org.uk

This consumer watchdog for the airline industry advises customers on their rights and helps them to bring an action. Click on Flight Plan and Got a Problem? for guidance.

Holiday Complaints

www.holidaycomplaints.com

This site is a useful source for checking to see whether travel operators have had complaints made against them. The database, although still in its infancy, is rather cumbersome, with a series of links before results are located. The site is limited to tour operators at the moment but within time they plan to introduce complaints against airlines, cruises, car rental and hotels. There is also useful advice on complaint procedure. Remember, there is no way of verifying whether these complaints are valid and the site is only as good as the number of people who contribute.

How to Complain

www.howtocomplain.com

This excellent site gives the user the tools to file a complaint online in a simple and efficient manner. Click on Transport and Travel and choose a category. From there, you will be pointed in the right direction, not only with good advice, but also an email link to the company that you wish to complain to.

PassengerRights.com
www.passengerrights.com

This American site takes you through the whole procedure of putting forward a complaint. By using their standard complaint form, taking their advice on how best to get results, PassengerRights will forward your email to the right person. Only a limited number of tour operators have put their names forward so before you go through the rigmarole of filing your grievance, check to see if the company is a participant.

CONSUMER REVIEWS

Ciao!
www.ciao.com

The travel section is comprehensive, with consumers airing their greivances, or singing their praises. If you have an idle moment, check out what you are letting yourself in for.

Dooyoo
www.dooyoo.co.uk

Share your opinion with fellow travellers on this consumer opinions platform. You can read honest reports on airlines, tour operators, hotels, and lots more. You just can't go wrong.

PASSPORTS AND VISAS

Post Office queues have become a distant memory as it is now possible to order the requisite forms for applying for a new passport via email. You can also find out what visas you may need for travel abroad, all from the comfort of your own home.

British Passport Office
www.ukpa.gov.uk

From this site, you can apply for the necessary application forms for a new British passport. Click on Travel Advice for information on visas for travellers entering the UK, and Urgent Applications for the procedures to follow if you need a passport within 48 hours or two weeks.

Embassy Web
www.embpage.org

The contact details of virtually every embassy in the world.

Fielding's Danger Finder
www.comebackalive.com/df

This site makes for essential reading if you are an intrepid traveller and like to get off the beaten track. Although flippant in manner, the site does have some very useful pieces of information.

Foreign & Commonwealth Office
www.fco.gov.uk/travel

This site holds the key to all the information you should know before departing on holiday. Advice on visas is given, along with travellers' tips. If necessary, check out If It All Goes Wrong to pinpoint the action you should take to make things better. A site to have tucked up your sleeve when the going gets tough.

Thames Consular Service

www.thamesconsular.com

A long-established independent passport and visa agency, operating in the UK and Europe. You can download visa forms, and order UK passports and even buy travel insurance.

PET TRAVEL

Dogs Away

www.dogsaway.co.uk

Now that you can travel with your cat or dog, this site provides invaluable information about taking Fifi and Fido on holiday.

VACCINATIONS

Find out what you might be letting yourself in for when visiting wilder parts of the world, and the action that you can take to prevent you bringing home more than you had bargained for.

e-med

www.e-med.co.uk

Of particular interest is the Travel Clinic, found in the tool bar at the top of the homepage. Email your intended destination and within four hours you will receive a report detailing the necessary jabs. The Immunisation Schedule outlines vaccine treatment and the length of cover. Medical packs can also be purchased from this site.

The Travel Doctor
www.tmvc.com.au/info10.html
This Australian site lists the necessary and recommended vaccinations needed when travelling to specific countries. Before information is released to you, you will have to agree to the Travel Health Advisory Report's conditions of use.

Tropical Medical Bureau
www.tmb.ie
Travellers Guide to Regions of the World gives advice on the jabs you will need for travelling to distant places. Information on the diseases to be found in these places, along with maps where cases are endemic, are also given.

INSURANCE
This is an area where you definitely need to read the small print. Policies differ greatly as well as prices. If you are covered for health through a group scheme, it is worth checking to see if that cover extends to travel for business as well as for holiday.

Columbus Direct
www.columbusdirect.net
An established company providing insurance to European users. Prices are competitive, not budget but the service is first-class.

Flynow
www.travel-bug.co.uk
Flynow uses travel insurance brokers Campbell Irvine Ltd, with underwriting from Lloyds. Click on Single Trip Travel Insurance to view coverage and use the Pricing Wizard for an instant quote.

GoSure

www.gosure.com

GoSure's site can give you a competitively priced instant quote, with reduced cost options such as no baggage and money cover.

Screentrade

www.screentrade

Screentrade are confident that they have the most competitive prices and offer to pay the difference if lower prices are found. Getting an instant quote is a little cumbersome but your personal details, once logged, are easily retrievable for future requests.

Travel Insurance Agency

www.travelinsurers.com

The TIA site quotes policy prices immediately without any input, making the site a good starting point when shopping around for a policy and they can also provide cover for British travellers who have already begun their journey.

CURRENCY

If you need to obtain funds in an emergency, MasterCard and Visa can come to your rescue. Do not forget that you will be charged commission for withdrawing funds on your credit card account.

Mastercard International Cardholder Services

www.mastercard.com/cardholderservices/atm/

This site informs travellers to the whereabouts of the Mastercard ATMs worldwide. It has sections on the uses of the card, such as acquiring travellers cheques and it lists the services that retailers are obliged to provide when they accept MasterCard.

OANDA
www.oanda.com/converter/travel
This is the only site to visit if you want to print out your own currency conversion chart. OANDA's cheat sheet is indispensable when shopping abroad, and what's more it is easy to use.

Visa
www.visa.com/pd/atm/
Another useful site for finding ATMs, the services that VISA offers, and travel safety recommendations. The ATM locators are fast and produce useful maps.

MAPS AND ROUTE PLANNERS
The internet is the perfect medium for printing out maps, which you can fold up and put into your handbag or pocket. The services offered just seem to be getting better and better.

Mapquest
www.mapquest.com
This site offers a door-to-door driving map service for Europe, the US, Canada and Mexico. Click on Driving Directions and fill in your request. Very detailed directions pop up, along with mileage and approximate travelling time.

Multimap
www.multimap.com
This site offers maps of Europe and the rest of the world. The searchable maps of the UK and America both turn up excellent quality whilst the European ones are a little less clear. The site boasts travel directions and a WAP service for mobile phones.

RAC
www.rac.co.uk
More than just RAC membership, this site offers a Route Planner that is free to all users. Enter your departure town and destination and wait for the results.

JUST FOR FUN

How far is it?
www.indo.com/distance
This brilliant page, on a site about Indonesia, will calculate the distance between two chosen destinations. Bring up the results with Map Viewer to illustrate where the two places are located.

TRAVEL INFORMATION: BOOKS AND MAPS
Every traveller needs a guide book and The Good Web Guide recommends the following publishers who specialise in travel books.

Stanfords
www.stanfords.co.uk
Since 1852, Stanfords, in London's Covent Garden, has been a destination shop for anyone wanting maps or travel books and accessories. Now their huge specialist range is available to all, through their online store. There's plenty here to tempt everyone from the armchair traveller through to intrepid explorer. The site is well-organised and efficient, although slow to load. Select Destination allows you to search their catalogue. Each category clicks through to a directory of maps, books and other items.

OTHER SITES OF INTEREST

Footprint
www.footprintbooks.com

Lonely Planet
www.lonelyplanet.com

Rough Guides
www.roughguides.com

AND FINALLY

World Time Server
www.worldtimeserver.com
This site will give you the time anywhere in the world in an instant. Bookmark it as you will find it incredibly useful if you frequently make international calls.

Cybercafes.com
www.cybercafes.com
Need to check your email or surf the net while abroad? Well log-on to this site before you leave home to find the net cafe nearest to where you are staying.

Index